D1082802

Curtis Aikens'
GUIDE TO THE
HARVEST

Curtis G. Aikens

Gramercy Books
New York

This 2002 edition is published by Gramercy Books, an imprint of
Random House Value Publishing, Inc., 280 Park Avenue, New York, NY 10017,
by arrangement with Peachtree Publishers, Ltd., Atlanta, Georgia.

Gramercy is a registered trademark and the colophon
is a trademark of Random House, Inc.

This is a revised edition of the Greengrocer's Guide to the Harvest,
published in 1991 by Peachtree Publishers, Ltd.

Printed in the United States of America

Random House
New York • Toronto • London • Sydney • Auckland
www.randomhouse.com

A catalog record for this title is available from the Library of Congress

ISBN: 0-517-22096-2

9 8 7 6 5 4 3 2 1

I can do all things through Christ, who strengthens me.

All of my work is dedicated to:

My parents, Laura B. Aikens and Eddie J. Aikens, Sr.,
who celebrated their forty-second anniversary May 12, 1993;

and

Dr. Martin Luther King, Jr., whose life's work and dreams
have allowed me to work and make my dreams come true.

This book and its author are dedicated to Curtis George Aikens, Jr.

On May 21, 1992, at 1:50 p.m. Pacific time, your mother and I welcomed you into our lives. I was
the first person to see you and the first person you saw. I loved you then, I love you now, and I will
love you forever.

Acknowledgments

This book would not be possible if hundreds of produce people in San Francisco, Oakland, New York, Atlanta, and other parts of the country had not been free with their knowledge and taught me their secrets to choosing fresh fruits and vegetables.

A very special thank you to the Marin County California Library and your literacy program, and especially to Jeni Hartman and Steve Seybold. I owe you a debt I doubt I can ever repay. Please keep teaching adults to read.

Thanks also to the editors of *The Rockdale Citizen,* Fred Turner and Tom Barry, for giving me a chance to write (and paying me!); and to Jack Lease, vice-president of WXIA-TV Atlanta, for caring about me and giving me a forum to share my knowledge of produce throughout the South.

Ruth Farmer, Margret Aikens, and Eileen Wischusen for correcting my spelling and putting up with all my mess.

Last, but certainly not least, Peachtree Publishers, old and new.

—1991

That's how the acknowledgments read for the first edition of my book, and those thoughts are still very much true. However, with a new edition comes a new set of acknowledgments.

I would like to thank the two executive producers I've worked with at ABC's "Home" show. First, Marty Ryan: thanks for hiring me and letting me share nationally my knowledge of produce and my passion for reading.

The other executive producer who created "Home" is Woody Fraser. We were friends long before we worked together, and although I don't know how long our working relationship will last, I know our friendship will last a lifetime. Man, you have been there for me.

Other people who have been, and are being, there for me are my dear friend Terry Handley and his wife, Wilma, both of whom I love deeply; Sue and Vince Lattanzio and their kids, Laurel and Luke; Mabel and Laura (Rabbit) Turrini; Peggie and Bala Kironde and their kids, Gibwa, Kagwa, and Tendo; Keith Stafford and Bonita (I'm praying things work out for you, and I love you both so much). During my darkest days, my northern California family members have brought light into my life.

Thanks also to my "Home" family. Sarah Purcell, you are a great friend. Gary Collins, thanks. Thanks to all the runners, especially Stephanie Rose, little Curtis's baby-sitter whenever he and I are at the show alone.

Special thanks to my attorney, Charles B. Tunnell, and to my former business attorney, Vincent E. Keys, for recommending you. You are an honorable person.

Dr. Sophie Darbonne Otis, thank you for teaching me the important lesson of life. I wish I had found you earlier.

I want to pass on my love to all the students I have spoken with or who have written me over the past few years. Remember, if I can do it, you can do it. And thanks to all the adult literacy groups I had the pleasure of working with; you all give me much more love than I could ever pass on.

Laura Goodman, associate editor of this book, you're a sweetheart. Emily Wright—"My Emily," as I call her around Peachtree—you're wonderful. I look forward to working with you again and again. And thanks again to Peachtree Publishers, old and new.

May my Lord bless and save you all. Catherine Laura Lehman, you are always loved.   —1993

CONTENTS

FRUITS

VEGETABLES

HERBS

NUTS

RECIPES

Preface

I remember years ago having lunch with Libby Staples, the publisher of the *Rockdale Citizen*, my hometown newspaper, which gave me my first chance to write. We were talking about how people can make you feel good, bad, happy, or sad. I said to Libby that if I had one wish, I would wish to spend five minutes with every person on earth, not just saying hello but spending five deep minutes, really letting that one soul share something with me, and, I hope, my soul would have something to pass on. I know that is a wish I will never be granted, so writing is the next best thing. I'd like to spend a few minutes with you right now, telling you about my background in the produce business, describing this book, and, most importantly, explaining why writing is so important to my being.

The only problem with "talking on paper" is that I don't get the pleasure of your response. However, you can write me, so please do, at P.O. Box 575, Conyers, Georgia 30207.

Why I Wrote This Book

I sold Peachtree Publishers on the idea of this book because, in my opinion, there is little in the way of straightforward information for consumers when it comes to selecting, storing, and using fresh fruits and vegetables. Do you know that the produce section is one of the most marked-up departments in the grocery store? It makes me mad to see shoppers getting ripped off every day! So one reason I've written this book is to give you the straight scoop on how to get the most for your produce dollar.

My second reason for writing this book is that I wanted to share with you some great recipes. I don't claim to be a world-class chef by any means. However, I do know my way around the kitchen, and I'm proud to say that there are some recipes in this book that I've prepared for some pretty famous people. So you may pick up a new trick or two if you read carefully.

When I was growing up, my dad said to me, "If information dies with you, it was never learned." I think that must be one of the old African-American sayings, because many of my ancestors couldn't read, so they passed on information verbally. This brings me to my final reason for writing this book, my hidden agenda for writing: There are more than 30 million adults in this great nation who cannot read, and until seven years ago I was one of them.

When I was growing up, my dad said to me, "If information dies with you, it was never learned." I think that must be one of the old African-American sayings, because many of my ancestors couldn't read, so they passed on information verbally.

From Illiteracy To Authorship

I know you are wondering, "How did this guy survive over a quarter of a century without knowing how to read, and why didn't he learn?" The why part is difficult to answer.

I come from a family of six kids: three boys and three girls. All of my siblings learned to read; they may not have been the best readers in their classes, according to my sister Sophia, but they could read. I couldn't.

I started school in 1965. Back then, throughout the South, including my hometown of Conyers, Georgia, the schools were separate, and supposedly equal. The African-American students, from grades 1 through 12, attended the J. P. Carr School, and the Anglo students attended one of three schools: Pine Street Elementary, Main Street, or Rockdale High.

I attended J. P. Carr for the first and second grades. These are the years when one gets a foundation in reading, and for some reason, whether it was lack of quality teaching, poor materials, or something else, I didn't get the basic skills one needs to develop into a reading person. And I knew it. Even at that early age, I was frustrated.

I had a friend who lived across the street, Danette Levett. She and I were the same age, but even though she was African American, she attended Pine Street, and she could read. My mother explained that Danette was able to go to Pine Street school because of what she called "freedom of choice." (This was about two years before the schools were totally integrated down South.) During the summer between the second and third grades, I told Mama I wanted to go to Pine Street and so did my sister, Sophia. To this day, I have no idea why Sophia wanted to attend that school, but for me the reason was perfectly plain: I wanted to get what Danette had—the ability to read.

So off I went to the third grade, excited about learning to read. My teacher, Mrs. Harper, was tough, I thought, but I still loved her, and I got along great with my classmates. I remember enjoying that year—until the last week of school, when Mrs. Harper had a meeting with Mama, with me present. Mrs. Harper and Mama included me in the discussion as my teacher explained to my mother how much she enjoyed having me in her class. She said that I worked hard and she had other nice things to say, too, which made me feel great. But then the roof caved in.

Mrs. Harper said to Mama that although I had made great progress that year at Pine Street, I was still behind my classmates in reading, and (the worst part for me) I should repeat the third grade.

I took Mrs. Harper's words to mean that I was dumb. *Now* I know that isn't what she meant, but you couldn't tell little Curtis Aikens that. And from that moment on, I swore no one would ever call me dumb again.

My cover-up started during my second year in the third grade. When the class would set up for reading time, our chairs were arranged in a huge semicircle. On the first day of the week, I would position myself right smack in the middle of my classmates. The reading would start on the right. Three, four, or five students would read, and then we'd stop and discuss the story. While my classmates were reading along in silence, I was listening very intently. I could remember the story almost word for word, so then I could lead the oral discussion. The next day I would move to the right, past the point where the reading had stopped the day before. Mrs. Redding would think that I had read the day before because I had been so vocal.

On those occasions when she would say, "Curtis, come on and read for us," I would get sick. I'd have a sudden stomachache or a sore throat—whatever it took to get out of class.

I passed third grade that year. For the fourth grade I went to a new school: Main Street. Miss Miles was my teacher, and this was her first year in the county. I remember a few times when I wanted to tell Miss Miles that I couldn't read, but I was afraid of being called "dumb," so I continued to keep my secret and to discover new ways to hide my inability to read. I became very good at memorizing things, and I always tried hard to make my teachers like me. I said things that I knew would please them, I participated actively in class discussions, and, being physically much bigger than my classmates, I got on my teachers' good side by keeping my classmates in line.

I think it was during those years that I truly understood the importance of my verbal skills. I realized that if you sound smart, people will think you are smart. I had always studied African-American television personalities such as Bill Cosby, Flip Wilson, Richard Pryor, Diahann Carroll, the Jackson Five, Lola Falana, and Sidney Poitier. The one thing they had in common was that none of them spoke with lazy tongues, as I call it. You could understand every word they said. I would also listen intently to music and radio deejays because they enunciated so very well. I learned about grammar and sentence structure over the radio and through television.

I remember my first day in high school like it was yesterday. As I walked to the entrance of Rockdale County High, I thought, "How in the world can I pull this off for four years?" But I made it. During my high school days, I was a member of the student council, president of the Minority Student Association, and one the most popular students in the school. I had a 30-hour-a-week job and was active in my community and church. I was well liked all over Rockdale County. I think I finished high school with a low C average. My teachers again thought I was lazy, or that I worked and practiced too much after school.

You see, by the time I graduated in 1978, I was a leader of the football team and was considered a standout in the region. When I was offered a football scholarship by Southern University in Louisiana, I thought it would give me a chance for a fresh start, and who knows—maybe in that predominantly African-American academic environment, I could finally disclose my secret.

While at Southern, I spoke with a university counselor. I was quite vague, saying only that I would love to be a better reader and dropping strong hints that I should be tested. I was put into a remedial class where I got very little instruction. When I spoke with someone about the lack of direction given in the class, I was told, "Oh, don't worry, you're a football player."

At that point, everything changed. My progress on the football field stopped, and my performance started to decline. I went from having a chance of starting to being "red-shirted," which meant that the following year, as far as

football was concerned, I would still be a freshman. Soon after that, I made the decision to run.

I transferred to the University of Georgia, intending to try out for football the following spring. But before spring practice came, I ran again. Some time before spring, a good friend and I took a cross-country trip. When we drove across the Arizona border into California, I had a feeling of homecoming. I felt I belonged out West. During that trip, I fell in love with two areas of the Golden State: San Diego and Marin County in the north.

After getting back to Georgia, I told my family I had heard the call—"Go West, young man"—and that's exactly what I was going to do. My dad drove with me as far as Oklahoma, where we visited my brother Jeffery. On a Sunday morning, I left Dad and Jeffery asleep in the hotel. I went out, started up the car, and thought to myself, "Where am I going, northern or southern California?" I decided to flip a coin: heads, Marin County; tails, San Diego. I flipped a quarter. When it landed in my hand, old George's face was looking at me. I thought for a split second "two out of three" but then said to myself, "No, I'm going to northern California."

It took me about three weeks to land a job. I was hired by Alpha Beta Stores, a large grocery chain on the West Coast. Things started out great. I made new friends, got to know the area, and made pretty good money. But before long I realized that I didn't want to work for a corporation. I am not just a number!

I decided I would make a living supplying restaurants with produce. I would go to all the restaurants in Marin County and say, "I can go to the farmer's market and buy and deliver your produce items with a little markup. By buying in volume for a number of restaurants I should get a better price, so you save money over shopping at the supermarket."

I named my company Peaches Produce, and I ran it for over five years. I think that at the height of my business I had 50 to 65 customers and was making lots of money. However, I was not happy inside. I lacked a feeling of self-worth; I suffered from low self-esteem, because I could not read.

With success comes competition. Eventually the larger produce suppliers in the area started taking aim at my accounts, offering them better prices. I started losing customers, and money. I didn't have the skills to write a business plan and present it to a bank, and by the time I was able to get all the paperwork filled out for Small Business Administration assistance, my business was gone.

The last year of Peaches was a rough time, and I was eating like a pig. Then, that same medium that taught me how to communicate verbally showed me that I was not the only person in the world who couldn't read.

One night I was watching television, stuffing my face with Coca-Cola and potato chips, when a public service announcement came on the air, saying, "If you have a reading problem, don't be ashamed or embarrassed. Call the literacy hotline. We can teach you." The most important aspect of the announcement, to me, was that the literacy hotline was confidential. No one had to know about my problem.

One night I was watching television, when a public service announcement came on the air, saying, "If you have a reading problem, don't be ashamed or embarrassed. Call the literacy hotline. We can teach you."

I put down my Coke and chips and made the call. Within weeks I was with my tutors, Steve Seybold and Jeni Hartman, whom I've come to love dearly. Less than eight months later, I was reading. I wasn't the very best reader in the world, but for the first time in my life I felt I was in control, or at least on the way to being in control. I didn't learn to read in time to save my business, but I did save my life.

Soon I moved to New York, and although I didn't like living in the Big Apple, I did learn a lot while I was there. From New York I traveled to Europe for the first time, and that was fascinating, too.

Then my family convinced me to move home to Conyers and start a new business. It was easy getting Aikens Family Produce, Inc., off the ground because I had done it before. We followed my business philosophy—"Low or no overhead means immediate *profits*"—and within a week we were making money.

During this time I took a trip down to Key West, where I had a chance to visit Ernest Hemingway's home. I had always loved hearing Hemingway's writing read out loud or seeing his books in movie form. I'd always wanted to express myself as Hemingway had on paper. I was up in his study totally alone when this powerful feeling came over me. I don't know whether it was the spirit of Mr. Hemingway or that of my Lord and Savior—probably both—but it was made clear to me that I had nothing to lose by trying to express myself on paper.

I don't know whether it was the spirit of Mr. Hemingway or that of my Lord and Savior— probably both— but it was made clear to me that I had nothing to lose by trying to express myself on paper.

When I got back to Conyers, I met with the editors of the local paper, Fred Turner and Tom Barry. I tried to talk them into letting me write a weekly column on fresh fruits and vegetables. I explained that I could give people information on how properly to select and store their fresh produce items, could tell them about the nutritional content of the food, and could give readers some historical background on the item of the week, as well as throw in stories about some of the rich and famous people I had met during the years I spent away from Conyers. Fred and Tom finally said, "Well, give us a sample column. We make no promises." They ran my column, the readers responded, and the paper even started to pay me for writing.

I really enjoyed writing my little column. I wrote some of my pieces in a question-and-answer format, and I came up with exciting ways of describing what most folks think of as boring vegetables, like swiss chard or turnips. Eventually I got the idea that I might be able to help other adults who could not read, so I wrote a little piece about the millions of nonreading Americans. Mail came pouring in.

Then I got a new idea. You know how everybody listens to celebrities when they are fighting for a cause, whether they believe in it or not? Well, I definitely believed in reading, and I knew about produce. Joe Carcione had passed away, so there was no one on television giving consumers advice about fresh produce. I decided to try to get on TV, figuring that if I could become well-known enough, I might be able to make a difference.

My friend Julie Mann Davis helped me get a spot on TV, and from that point on, I totally dedicated myself to the literacy movement in this country.

At this point in time, I'd say that my plan is working. I have become a published author; the first version of this book, *The Greengrocer's Guide to the Harvest*, was released in 1991. I've also been featured on NBC's "Nightly News," ABC's "World News Tonight," CNN, "Entertainment Tonight," "Good Morning America," and the front page of *USA Today*. I've been to the White House twice and have become a regular member of ABC Daytime's "Home" show.

Please don't take all this as a boast. The point is that because of the exposure I've gotten, I'm able to help nonreaders find programs all across this great country that will help them to read. My success on television also reinforces that belief that, "if you read, you can succeed."

There are quite a few things in my life that give me pride, and about at the top of that list was the day I was able to record a public service announcement for ABC, because that marked the day I had come full circle. It had been seven years earlier that I had seen the public service announcement that saved my life.

Cooking With Curtis

When I wrote the first version of this book, I based it on the produce descriptions I had written for the Rockdale Citizen. The first version included some recipes, but my main goal in writing the book was to provide consumers with solid information about the history, storage, selection, and nutritional content of fruits and vegetables.

In this revised edition, I have added some new produce descriptions, but mostly I've added lots of yummy new recipes. All of the new recipes are vegetarian, though I've kept the meat recipes that I originally had in the book.

I cut red meat out of my diet twelve years ago, and two years ago I cut *all* meat out of my diet, even fish. At first I became a vegetarian in an effort to lose weight. It didn't work; I'm still fat—or maybe "big" would be a kinder description. But I found out that when you don't have meat to stick on the plate, you become a more creative cook. Not having meat to use in preparing meals forced me to come up with some exciting and very healthy vegetarian meals, and I'm eager to share my new recipes with you.

As for my experience as a cook, I started out trying to emulate my mother. As a young boy, I loved watching her prepare meals, from selecting items at the store to tossing the salad and "picking greens" (getting them ready to cook) and stringing beans, even cutting up chicken. And of course, I especially enjoyed watching her fry chicken.

I always thought my mother was the best cook in the world, so I started out trying to emulate her. My cooking started with a phone call to Mama when I was living away from home. I told her I would love to have some of her fried chicken, so she told me how to make it myself. After a few attempts, I got pretty good at frying chicken. Then I started getting weekly installments from Mama. I think banana pudding was next, then cornbread, then black-eyed peas—

I found out that when you don't have meat to stick on the plate, you become a more creative cook. Not having meat to use in preparing meals forced me to come up with some exciting and very healthy vegetarian meals.

and before I knew it I was having friends over and cooking down-home country meals.

Those meals were just as fattening where I was living as they are down south, and pretty soon I had blown up to 350 pounds. At that point I stopped eating red meat and started thinking about the way I cooked other foods. I cut down on butter and stopped using lard altogether.

All of this brings me to a question a reader once asked me that will help you understand my approach to cooking: "What's your culinary philosophy?"

When I got that letter, it made me laugh. I thought to myself, "Ha! I'm from Conyers, Georgia. I can't have a philosophy!" So I didn't answer that person, but the question keeps coming up in different forms: "What's your aim in the kitchen?" or "How do you develop recipes?" or "What are your thoughts on the culinary arts?" Eventually I started giving this question serious thought.

As I said, I started out emulating my mother, but over the years I've found myself trying to bridge the gap between down-home country cooking, with all that flavor, and California nouveau cuisine, which is pleasing to the eye and healthy for the body. I try to develop recipes that are easy to prepare, taste great, are filling, and are good for you. I don't have a name for it yet, but that's my philosophy. I hope you like the recipes that come from it, and if you want a total vegetarian cookbook from yours truly, write and let me know.

Introduction

Becoming a Better Garden Grocer

When I broke into the produce business way back when, I thought I knew everything there was to know about fresh fruits and vegetables. You see, as a little boy, I was always around produce. My grandfather, W. H. Curtis, Sr., was the best farmer I ever saw, which brings me to the first term I would like to talk about—*organic*. Granddaddy, like most of the old-timers, farmed organically long before we knew of nitrates leaching into our soil, the potential effects of alar, and pesticide residues. Granddaddy thought that the old way was the best way. I can remember him saying, "I've seen lots of collard greens grown with bag fertilizer, but I ain't never seen any as good as mine, and I know they don't taste better." My dictionary says "organically grown" means using fertilizer and mulches consisting only of animal or vegetable matter with no chemical fertilizers or pesticides. That's the way Granddaddy did it, and he did it cost effectively.

Never settle for limp, dried-looking produce. Demand top quality, fresh and alive-looking produce.

With that in mind, when shopping for organic fruits and vegetables, never settle for limp, dried-looking produce. Demand top quality, fresh and alive-looking produce. If an organic retailer tells you the produce looks bad because the farmer can't use pesticides, then you politely inform him or her that the supplier isn't much of an organic farmer.

One more Granddaddy story: He used to apply a white, milky-looking liquid to his garden. He didn't have a fancy name for it. He just referred to it as a lime mix. Nowadays, it is called Bordeaux, and it is making a strong impact on the modern organic farmers.

You may never see the next few terms listed in the produce section or featured in any written advertisements, but knowing them and what they stand for will help you select fresher and sweeter produce. This knowledge will also save you money.

When I started to shop for wholesale produce, I thought an apple was an apple; a mushroom, a mushroom; and a zucchini, a zucchini. I had no idea a single produce item could be graded into one of no less than four categories. "Extra fancy" is the highest grade. Then comes "fancy," "choice," and finally "mature," sometimes referred to as "number two." I learned those categories and what they stood for relatively quickly, thanks to people like Joe Carcione, Pat Murphy, and Charlie Bettencourt. All were men that I knew while buying in the Golden Gate Produce Terminal in south San Francisco. Each separately took me under his wing and shared his knowledge of the produce world. Before that, I would buy what I thought was top grade, only to discover later I should have paid much less. The following grade levels are not USDA standards. They are trade terms that the men and women of the produce industry have devised over the years to discuss size, color, and quality of fresh fruits and vegetables among themselves.

Going from bottom to top, we'll start with **mature.** A good produce person will never say he has some bad produce to sell; however, he will say, for instance, "I have some number two mushrooms, or soup tomatoes I'm sure you could put to use." Remember, just because these items are our lowest grade does not mean the produce is bad or inedible. For example, number two mushrooms should not always be passed by. These mushrooms are mature and full-flavored, which makes them excellent for sauces and on pizzas. The soup tomato is another mature item that is too soft for sandwiches but excellent in soup and other cooked dishes.

The next produce grade level is **choice.** Vegetables with this grade level are usually considered irregular, be it size or shape; however, the taste is normally as good as any of the top grades. Fruits with this grade usually show slight blemishes. For the consumer on a close budget, the choice items could be your best shopping value.

The top two grades, **fancy** and **extra fancy,** are very hard to tell apart in fruits. With apples, for instance, an extra fancy apple shows 90 to 100 percent color. In other words, a red apple is completely red or close to it. Fancy apples show 75 to 90 percent color, although the taste is virtually the same. But the price could range from a difference of ten to twenty cents per pound.

Now in vegetables, these grades of fancy and extra fancy usually stand for size, fancy being medium-sized. I'll use a zucchini for our measuring stick: a fancy would be six to eight inches long and from one and one-half to two inches around; an extra fancy would be four to six inches long and no more than an inch and one-half around. Small vegetables usually bring much higher price tags in most markets. However, taste does not vary much between fancy and extra fancy vegetables.

Now that you are familiar with some of the produce industry's inside grade levels and what they mean, I want you to know what I think are the four keys needed to unlock the door to becoming an expert greengrocer. These keys should guide you through any produce section, helping you choose the freshest and sweetest fruits and vegetables available. One or more of these keys will always come into play in selecting fresh fruits or vegetables.

(1) **LOOK.** Always look at your fresh fruit or vegetable to be sure it has good color. However, color is not always a true indication of ripeness. The main things to look for are bruises or scars. If either is present, disregard that item and choose one free from damage. Why? Let's face it: pesticides and other chemicals are with us to stay, and in most instances they are applied to the outside of produce. Although they can't be washed away, they can be peeled away, but if scars or bruises are present, that pesticide on the outside may seep into the flesh of your fresh fruit item. So remember, avoid damaged produce.

(2) **SMELL.** Don't be afraid to follow your nose. Here is something I will never forget. Once while shopping in New York's Hunt's Point Market, two so-called produce experts laughed at me for smelling tomatoes. I not only got upset,

I got mad. I pointed out to those guys that the boxes I did not select were bad. If they would smell they could tell. I also pointed out to the "experts" that as tomatoes ripen, they do give off a rather strong tomato aroma. Which brings up another good saying about fruits: If it smells peachy, it's going to taste peachy. Remember, as fruit ripens, not only does the sugar level rise, but also the fragrance becomes much stronger and more fruity. As for vegetables, when they pass their peak, they usually give off a slightly sour smell.

(3) **TOUCH.** No buyer of fresh fruit wants items that are either rock-hard or marshmallow soft. Most fruit, when ripe, gives just a little to slight pressure. Remember that it's okay to pick up produce and inspect it before buying, but please do not squeeze the life out of items, especially ones that you are not going to purchase. A piece of fruit that was too hard or too soft for your liking may be just perfect for someone else. Vegetables, be they broccoli, cabbage, carrots, or whatever, should always be firm. Never buy limp vegetables.

(4) **SEASON.** Know the season of fresh fruits and vegetables and buy what is in season. You will learn the seasons while reading this book; the buying part is up to you. However, each year selecting fruits and vegetables in season becomes more difficult due to ever-increasing shipments of fresh fruits and vegetables from the southern hemisphere, where the seasons are the opposite of ours. Before buying an item from a region with a reverse season, first see what that region has to offer.

One easy way to tell what is in season is to take a moment to look around your greengrocer's store or the produce section of your supermarket and see which items are in the greatest abundance.

I guess I should add a fifth key: get to know your greengrocer, who should be able to tell you anything there is to know about the produce in his or her shop. And if one greengrocer can't, find a new one.

A further note: Although fresh fruits and vegetables will often keep a week in the refrigerator, it is best to use them within three days of purchasing. And in most cases, storing them in paper bags is preferable to storing in plastic ones.

Wax Coating on Produce

There is nothing new about waxing fresh produce. Most people don't realize that the first coating is applied by Mother Nature herself to protect the produce against hot sunlight and to retain moisture. Even when shopping for true organic produce, you may notice a fine layer of wax present on fruits and vegetables. You need not worry; that wax is a sign of freshness. The only way to get fresher produce would be to pick it from the garden yourself.

As for human beings waxing produce, there's nothing new about that either. The Chinese have been waxing fruits for hundreds of years. For most of

Nature applies wax to produce for protection; processors do so to enhance appearance and, more importantly, to extend the shelf life of fruits and vegetables.

the twentieth century in America, processing houses have coated various produce items with a petroleum-based wax (with FDA approval), with waxing ranging from very fine on fruits like apples and grapes to quite thick on certain root vegetables like rutabagas, turnips, and some beets.

Nature applies wax to produce for protection; processors do so to enhance appearance and, more importantly, to extend the shelf life of fruits and vegetables. Waxed produce is the main reason I advise against buying bruised fruits. As long as the fruit is undamaged, the wax is confined to the skin and can be removed, but if the item is bruised, the wax may seep into the flesh and in turn be consumed by you or your children. Remember, the wax is FDA approved, but if you are like me, you want to be careful about how much petroleum-based product you have floating around inside your body.

How can you remove wax from produce? Neither natural nor artificial wax can be rinsed off in cold water, but nature's coating will evaporate on its own, and wax additives can be removed in very warm water. However, the best way to ensure that no wax is consumed is to peel the produce. Don't stop buying fresh fruits because of waxing.

Curtis Aikens'

Guide to the Harvest

Fruits

Vegetables

Herbs

Nuts

FRUITS

Apples

Once the forbidden fruit, the apple is now the most preferred. There have been more than seven thousand varieties documented since that infamous incident in the Garden of Eden. Out of those many varieties, the best-known and best-selling of all time is the **Red Delicious.** It's the perfect-looking apple, beautiful in color and quite shapely, and it has a nice, sweet flavor. Although no other apple may be as pretty as the Red Delicious, you can find many other varieties far superior in flavor.

Starting with the green varieties, there are two that stand out in my mind and on my tastebuds. While living in northern California, I was invited to a wine and cheese tasting out in the Napa Valley. The wine was good, but what caught my attention was the apple being served on the cheese tray. No one at the tasting could tell me the name of the little, green, tomato-shaped apple until I found the gardener, who took me out to the orchard. He said the apple was a **Pippin** and that it's much better for cooking than eating out of hand. I found that hard to believe until I made my mom's apple pie using the Pippin. Here's that recipe if you would like to try it (but you can use any variety of apples to make her pie).

AVAILABLE
year-round

DOMESTIC PEAK
August-October

MOM'S EASY APPLE PIE

Add apples to crust; pour sugar and nutmeg over apples; slice margarine and arrange in pan; cover with sheet of dough and prick in several places; bake for 45 to 55 minutes at 375 degrees.

3-4 medium apples peeled, cored, and sliced
1 cup sugar
1/4 tsp. nutmeg
1/2 stick margarine
1 homemade pie crust

The Pippin apple may be hard to find on the East Coast, but if you can find it, try it.

The other green apple I love is the **Granny Smith.** Each year this apple takes more and more of the American market than any apple since the Red Delicious. By the year 2000, the Granny Smith may be the world's most popular apple. These apples are light green and when fully ripened have a yellow tint up near the stem end. This apple is crisp and has a tart, sweet flavor. I love the Granny Smith apple.

Another good apple is the **McIntosh:** this apple can't decide whether it's red or green, so let's call it two-toned. The McIntosh is juicy and tender, not too sweet, but sweet enough. The flesh is snow-white and makes nice applesauce. The McIntosh is probably the second best baking apple.

The best baking apple is the **Rome Beauty.** This big boy can take the heat in the oven and won't collapse or lose its shape. Some experts describe this apple as having very little flavor, but I, on the other hand, truly enjoy its taste, which is faintly sweet. One of the things I love about Romes is that they are very crunchy to bite.

Other apples you may want to try include:

Winesap: Growers aren't producing as many Winesaps as in years past. This is a mystery to me because this firm, dark, red-skinned, yellow-fleshed apple is sweet, with a flavor that reminds me of homemade wine.

Mutsu: Imported from Japan, it is crisp, juicy, and very sweet. Some say this is the perfect apple. The Mutsu sometimes grows to be as large as a melon. It is now being grown on the West Coast and is being marketed under the name Fuji Apple. I am sure this apple will become quite popular before long.

Rhode Island Greenie: It is tough to get, but if you want the best for your family, and if you take the time to bake homemade pies, cook with this apple.

Other apples that are hard to find, but worth the hunt are **Jonathan** red apples, grown in the Northeast, with yellow flesh and a sweet flavor; the **Empire,** an upstate New York apple that is crisp and crunchy; and the **Gravenstein,** another two-toned apple grown out west. This last apple will rank with any as far as flavor is concerned, though it isn't much to look at.

Apples are available year-round, but the peak season is August through October. Select apples that are bruise-free and firm to the touch. Refrigerate apart from strong-smelling foods. Apples are rich in vitamins A, B, and C, as well as fiber, iron, and potassium.

Apricots

Like its relatives, nectarines and peaches, apricots are native to China. Cots (a common name for apricots) originated some three to four thousand years ago. The fruit made its way west through Europe and became very popular in the Mediterranean. It's believed that some of the first settlers brought apricots to America; however, the fruit didn't do well on this continent until the 1700s, when Spanish padres planted apricots throughout California as they opened new missions. At one point during the 1970s, California produced over 85 percent of the apricots grown in the United States as well as accounting for at least 45 percent of the worldwide output.

AVAILABLE
May-August

DOMESTIC PEAK
July-August

This fragile fruit is almost as pleasant to look at as it is to taste. From the reddish-orange skin of the **Katy** variety to the bright orange of the **Tilton,** the apricot is a beautiful fruit.

Apricots reach their peak flavor when allowed to tree ripen, so you probably won't get to taste apricots at their best unless you have an apricot tree in your backyard. When ripe, the apricot is the most fragile of all summer fruits. Therefore, very few, if any, ripe apricots are shipped to wholesale or retail markets.

With that in mind, select firm fruit when shopping, for it will ripen at room temperature in two or three days and achieve a full and pleasant flavor. However, as with other summer fruits, color is the key. If the fruit was harvested before obtaining a full orange or red blush, it is very likely to become sour or to shrivel before it softens and ripens.

Not too long ago, only a few apricot varieties were sold in retail outlets: ***Royal, Derby, Stewart,*** and ***Blenheim.*** The four are so similar in appearance and taste that they are marketed under the same name, Royals. The original Royal was brought over from France in 1850 and was planted in northern California in the Winters area, which produces more apricots than any other single area in the world. Today there are many varieties making quite an impact on the market, such as the Katy, the ***Patterson,*** and the improved ***Flaming Gold,*** just to name a few. The new hybrid varieties are bigger and have strong colors, but their flavors just cannot surpass the Royal varieties. The season for fresh apricots runs May through August, peaking July through August.

Remember, firm apricots will ripen in two or three days on your countertop. Then store them in the refrigerator until you are ready to eat them. The apricot is a good source for vitamin A and contains some vitamin C. For the calorie-conscious, one fresh apricot contains only about twenty calories.

Avocados

AVAILABLE
Year-round

I call avocado my California fruit because I had never tasted one until I moved out west. However, the picture writing of the Aztec and Mayan civilizations proves that this native American crop was being consumed long before Columbus made his way west. The pictures date to 300 B.C., but the avocado did not appear in North America until the nineteenth century. This nonsweet fruit (yes, the avocado is a fruit, although many produce people discuss them as if they were vegetables) was first planted in Florida during the 1830s. That same century, Spanish missionaries introduced the avocado to California.

The avocado industry began around the turn of the twentieth century in both Florida and California. However, the two states produce two very different types of avocados. The Florida avocado came from eastern South America and the West Indies. In Florida, as in the islands, the soil is much looser, the rainfall heavier, and the humidity higher than in California. In these conditions, the fruit grows to a much larger size, but also has a higher water content, resulting in a less nutty flavor than its California counterpart. Some of the popular Florida varieties are **Walden, Booth,** and **Lula,** but in stores they are usually marketed under one name: Florida avocado. The California avocado, thanks to climate, has thicker skin, a richer, thicker texture, and, of course, a less watery content. The flavor is quite nutty. Some say eating California avocados is like drinking fresh brewed coffee, whereas Florida avocados are like instant decaf.

To cut the ripening time of avocados in half, add a tomato to the bag.

Here are some California varieties:

The **Bacon** looks very much like a Florida avocado. During the early days of Peaches Produce, I got into a few verbal fights over that large, pitted, watery, smooth-skinned variety. I just refused to pay the wholesaler the California price for what I thought was a Florida avocado. I had to make some apologies when I learned the Bacon was indeed from the West Coast.

The **Zutano** is medium-sized like the Bacon, but with more of a pear shape. It is available in markets from late fall through the winter. In the produce business, it's called a winter variety.

The **Fuerte** was the only variety not wiped out during the California freeze of 1913. In Spanish, *fuerte* means "strong." The Fuerte is by far the most popular winter avocado. If you're not careful, you could mistake it for a green Bosc pear. This variety, with medium-thick skin and a mild, nutty flavor, is second only to the Hass variety.

I've saved the best for last—the **Hass**. This oval-shaped beauty is in season from April through late November. The bumpy, thick green skin darkens as the fruit ripens until it's a shiny jet black. The flavor, unsurpassed anywhere, is very rich, walnutty, and quite oily—so oily that out west many people use avocados as a skin conditioner.

Until recently avocados were thought of as exotic or as a food for the rich and famous, but now, thanks to the California Avocado Commission and increased production, consumers from all walks of life enjoy this richly nutritional fruit. The avocado supplies high amounts of vitamins A, B, and C, and it is loaded with potassium. However, California avocados are also high in fat and calories. With that in mind, you may want to consider the Florida varieties, which have about half the calories and fat. I should point out that avocado fat is not concentrated, so it is not as unhealthy as palm fat or animal fat.

California avocados have a twelve-month season, compared to an eight-month season in Florida. Florida avocados are not available during spring. When shopping, remember that as with pears and bananas, avocados never reach their flavorful peak until after they have been harvested; they do not ripen fully on the tree. This is an advantage because it means you can control the ripening of your own fruit. Always select hard green fruit free of cuts. When you take them home, place them in a brown paper bag and put the bag in a warm spot. (I always put mine on top of my refrigerator.) Check them daily, for they will ripen fast: Florida varieties take three to four days, and the Californias, four to six days. To cut the ripening time in half, add a tomato to the bag. The natural gases released by the tomato speed up the process.

I enjoy avocados in three special ways: I love them sliced on crackers or sliced with tomatoes and onions (no dressing needed), but guacamole is my all-time favorite way to eat avocados. Here is a guacamole recipe I got from Eddie and Mary Ayub in San Diego:

GUACAMOLE

Peel and pit avocados. Slice into a bowl, mash up, mix in lemon juice, mayonnaise, and onion. If you like hot things add ground jalapeño or finger pepper. Diced tomatoes or salsa are also great.

3 avocados
juice from 1 lemon
1/2 tbs. mayonnaise
1 medium onion,
    diced

Bananas

The banana originated in southern Asia, where it was being harvested as food long before most other fruits. Columbus introduced the banana plant to the American tropics, where it thrived. In fact, later explorers believed the plant was native to the western hemisphere.

AVAILABLE
year-round

Believe it or not, bananas are the world's most popular . . . *berry!* Something else you won't believe is that they don't grow on trees; rather, they grow on giant tropical herbs that look like trees. The botanical name of the berry borne by this giant herb is *musa sapientum,* which means "fruit of the wise men." To us they are more commonly known as bananas, the third most popular fruit in America, ranking just behind apples and oranges.

Most folks say a banana is a banana, and that's pretty much true, but there are two types sold in the United States: the **Cavendish,** which has a flat, blunt end, and the **Gros Michel,** which has kind of a pointed end. This is the only way to tell the two apart; they taste the same. However, there are some new bananas on the scene that you should put on your buy-and-try list: first, red bananas (red Spanish or red Cuban), and second, little finger bananas, also known as apple bananas. When I worked at Balducci's in New York City, one of our best accounts was the United Nations dining facility, which of course caters to many international diplomats, one of whom was former Secretary of State George Schultz. Mr. Schultz loves bananas, and I'm told his favorite is the little finger banana. Whenever Mr. Schultz was in New York, the UN chef would call up and say, "Curtis, the Secretary's coming," and I knew it was time to round up the little finger bananas.

Because they are a tropical fruit, bananas are available year-round and normally sell at reasonable prices. When shopping, choose fruits with an even yellow color. They are perfect for eating and will keep two or three days at room temperature. You can store bananas in the refrigerator, but only after they are ripened; the skin will darken, but the flesh will still taste great.

As for nutrition, bananas are loaded with vitamin A and contain some vitamins B and C. Low in fat, they are a good source for calcium, iron, and phosphorus, and of course, they're an excellent source for potassium, containing 260 milligrams of potassium per banana—and only eighty-eight calories.

Carambola

AVAILABLE
*September-
January*

The **Star Fruit** is an exotic and beautiful fruit with a unique appearance. Native to Malaysia, it now grows very well in Hawaii and the islands of the Caribbean. You can find some star fruit from Florida and California, but remember, the best comes from the tropical regions because the trees are very sensitive to the cold. The flavor of the star fruit ranges from tart and sweet to very sour, depending on variety and ripeness. Your produce person should be able to tell you the name of the variety that is carried in that shop. The sweetest variety is the **Gold Star** when fully ripe. Unripe carambola are pale yellow, have very little flavor, or are very sour. As the fruit ripens, the color changes to a rich, dark yellow, and the flavor becomes much sweeter.

The season for carambola is September through January. The key to selecting this exotic fruit is color, which should be dark and yellow—and be sure to ask your produce person for the Gold Star variety. Most star fruits are eaten raw, or in a fruit salad; they may also be chilled inside gelatin, and although I have never tried it this way, I was told by a food stylist in Los Angeles that star fruit is very tasty when sautéed in rosé wine.

The carambola is extremely high in vitamin A and quite low in calories and fat.

Cherimoya

I once received a letter which said, "While traveling in South America, I ate this strange fruit that looked like a dark artichoke, with black seeds inside. My traveling companion called it custard fruit. Do you know what it is?"

The fruit that the curious traveler wrote about is indigenous to South America; it is native to the cool regions of the Andes Mountains of Peru and Bolivia. It is the cherimoya.

The cherimoya is something special. Although I had never heard it referred to as custard fruit, I have heard it called **custard apple.** The flavor is the special part of this exotic fruit, a mixture of banana, pineapple, and, some say, pear. The texture does remind me of custard pie.

The letter contained a perfect description of the ripened fruit; however, since the cherimoya is extremely delicate when ripe, probably few shoppers have seen one in that condition.

When shopping for cherimoya, you should look for a light-green, pear-shaped fruit which at first glance makes you think there is something wrong with this artichoke. The best thing to do is to ask your produce person for cherimoya. Although cherimoya is

AVAILABLE
*November-
April*

being grown in California on a fairly large scale, it is still considered quite exotic and is also very expensive in the United States. You probably won't find them at your local supermarket unless enough shoppers demand them.

The season begins in November and ends in April. Fresh cherimoya makes an excellent addition to any fruit salad, and it will give your guests something to talk about. Eating cherimoya out of hand can be quite trying because of the large, inedible black seeds. I suggest cutting the fruit into quarters, removing the seeds with a knife or fork, then scooping out the flesh with a spoon to eat on the spot or to add to salad.

A medium cherimoya contains about ninety calories, like an apple. It is also a good source of vitamins A and C as well as iron and phosphorus. Well-rounded, I'd say.

Coconuts

AVAILABLE
year-round

The coconut has been cultivated for so long in the tropical regions of the world that no one has an exact fix on its birthplace. Like its cousin, the date, the coconut is produced on palm trees. Just as the date palm is highly regarded in the desert regions of the world, the coconut palm is equally prized in the tropics, not just for the food it produces but also for its by-products. Some of the by-products of the coconut palm include soaps, margarines, ropes, mats, and many other items. The real prize is the milky white flesh of the coconut itself. I love to enjoy fresh coconut as a snack, and it is also great grated over fruit salads. Fresh coconut comes to U. S. markets from many areas, including the Dominican Republic and Puerto Rico. It is available year-round but is most abundant during the fall and winter.

When selecting fresh coconut, simply pick it up and shake it.

If you hear a sloshing sound, you have a winner. If not, the coconut is dried out and the flesh may be dry and no good.

There must be seven or eight techniques for opening a coconut, but all of them involve poking out one or two of the dark brown spots, called eyes, located at the top of the nut. After poking out the eyes, drain the liquid, which may be chilled and enjoyed as a drink or added to other beverages to enhance taste. Then place the nut on a hard surface and hit it squarely between the eyes with a hammer or, as the early Hawaiians did, with a big rock; a split should occur right down the middle. Simply pry open your coconut and pull the flesh away from the shell. There are two other methods of opening a coconut: first, you may freeze it, which makes the hard shell much more brittle, so that it cracks easily when struck by a hammer; or you may place the drained coconut in a preheated 400-degree oven for fifteen to twenty minutes until it cracks open.

Coconuts will keep for months, as long as you don't poke out the eyes. Like most of the other hard fruits (nuts), coconuts are also quite high in calories. However, this bodybuilding fruit is a good source for protein, iron, and phosphorus.

MAMA IN-LAW'S COCONUT PIE

Melt chocolate with butter over low heat. Gradually blend in milk and set aside. Mix sugar, cornstarch, and salt. Beat in eggs and vanilla. Gradually blend in chocolate mixture. Pour into pie shell. Combine coconuts and nuts. Sprinkle over pie. Bake at 350 degrees for 45-50 minutes or until set. Cover with foil for the last 15 minutes of baking. Let sit 4 hours before serving. Freezes well.

1 4-oz. package semi-
   sweet chocolate
1/4 cup butter
1-2/3 cup evaporated
   milk
1-1/2 cup sugar
3 Tbl. cornstarch
1/8 tsp. salt
2 eggs
1 tsp. vanilla
1 unbaked 9" pie shell
   (deep dish)
1-1/3 cup coconut
1/2 cup pecans,
   chopped

Dates

Fresh dates can be traced back to about 3500 B.C. In the Middle East, where dates were first cultivated, every part of the fruit was used. Date cakes were made from the meat, honey from the juice, and oil from the seed. Not only was the fruit a great prize because of its many uses, but the palm tree on which it grew was equally valuable. The center of the date palm could be pounded into flour, and a rather potent alcoholic beverage was brewed from the sap. The leaves were used in many ways, and the fiber was made into very strong rope.

Dates were introduced to North America by the Spanish missionaries along the California and Mexican coastlines; however, the date palm did not thrive on this continent until the early part of this century, when Dr. W. T. Swingle brought an Algerian variety *(Deglet Noor,* which means "date of the night") to the deserts of Southern California, where the city of Indio stands today, in the Coachella Valley.

More than one hundred varieties are grown in California alone, but of all those varieties, one accounts for 95 percent of the total annual date sales in the United States. This is the same variety Dr. Swingle introduced some eighty years ago, the Deglet Noor.

The Deglet Noor is a semidry date. When ripe, it is amber in color and very tasty. You may want to try others, but be aware that they are hard to find. Two of these are the *Medjool,* a rather large, attractive sweet date, and the *Barhi,* the softest and most delicate of the dates.

Fresh dates make an excellent out-of-hand snack and are also nice to bake with. Mix in some chopped fresh dates the next time you make banana bread, or when a recipe calls for nuts, substitute dates. They are also good to mix in when making homemade candies.

Fresh dates are available starting in May, and the season winds down in September. When shopping, choose dates that are high in color and moist and soft to the touch. Remember, dry fruit is old fruit. The fruit will keep for weeks wrapped in plastic in the refrigerator.

Dates are very nourishing and are loaded with potassium, calcium, iron, and phosphorus. However, like nuts, they are high in calories.

Figs

This is one of the oldest fruits known, if not the oldest. The fig originated in Asia, and as humanity branched out from that Garden of Eden, so too did this ancient fruit. Turkey, Greece, and Italy all became home to this wonderful food item. To this day, figs remain a major crop in all of those countries. However, it was the Spanish who introduced the fig to America, and some of the world's best and most flavorful are now grown in California.

AVAILABLE
June-November

DOMESTIC PEAK
September-October

It's a shame that most of the figs sold retail in the United States are dried, because those who have tried fresh figs know how sweet and juicy and refreshing they are. There are many varieties of figs, but only two basic types: light (green and/or white) and dark (black or deep purple). I think the dark varieties offer the best flavor. If you're not a fresh fig eater, it's time to become one.

For first-timers, I recommend the **Mission Fig,** sometimes called the **Black Mission.** The skin color is such a deep purple it looks black, and the flesh is pink and, oh, so sweet. The Mission is my favorite, and it's also the leading commercial type. After you fall in love with the Mission, try the **Brown Turkey Fig,** another of the dark varieties, with soft red flesh that is rich in flavor.

Calimyrnas are large figs three to four inches in diameter, and **Kodota** is a violet-fleshed fig; both are excellent light varieties to start with. Both have a nice, sweet flavor and are quite juicy.

When shopping for fresh figs, choose fruits soft to the touch and dark in color—deep purple or black in the dark varieties and golden yellow in the light ones. Color and softness are good signs of peak flavor and ripeness. Fresh figs are available June through November, with the season peaking in September and October.

Nutritionally, figs are good energy food, so instead of a candy bar, try a fresh fig. They are an excellent source of sugar but are low in calories, containing only about fifty per large fig. Keep in mind that figs and vanilla ice cream make a wonderful dessert. However, my favorite way to enjoy a fresh fig is simply to slice it and eat it.

Grapefruit

AVAILABLE
year-round

**DOMESTIC
PEAK**
*September-
July*

As recently as eighty years ago, the grapefruit was all but unknown outside Florida. The parent of today's grapefruit is called **pomelo;** like the other members of the citrus family, it originated in Asia. The pomelo was about twice the size of a large modern grapefruit, had thick puffy skin, and was very sour and filled with seeds. During the late seventeenth century, a sailor named Shaddock transplanted some pomelo seeds to the West Indies (later pomelos were also known as Shaddocks), and around the same time a former officer in the French navy planted pomelo seeds in Florida, laying the foundation for the world's best and largest production area for the grapefruit.

One hundred years before the pomelo, a sour citrus, was introduced to the New World, the mandarin orange, a sweet citrus, had become well established. Within forty years of the pomelo's introduction to the same tropical regions, cross-pollination took place between the sweet and sour citrus, yielding a new, unnamed fruit. Too sour to be an orange, yet too sweet to be a pomelo, this new fruit was small and grew in clusters like grapes on a vine. That's where the name "grapefruit" came from.

It's funny that this once unnamed fruit is now being grown the world over. Producing countries include Greece, Spain, Cuba, Brazil, and Israel. However, none of those countries can match the output and quality of homegrown grapefruits. The United States leads in production, with Florida being the main producer, followed by Texas, California, and Arizona. As for which are the best-tasting, the Texas growers claim that none are as sweet and juicy as their beautiful, sunset-tinted, pink- or red-fleshed grapefruits (the first citrus to be patented). Texas grapefruits are marketed under several names: ***Pink Marsh, Thompson, Ruby,*** and ***Ruby Red.*** They are all something special.

On the other hand, without Florida there would be no grapefruit industry. As I said, during the early part of this century the only people to taste grapefruit were those who had visited Florida. When the growers finally began shipping their new fruit to regions outside Florida, they were pleasantly surprised with sales figures. Today the Sunshine State not only leads in production and sales, accounting for nearly 80 percent of America's annual crop, but the state also leads in world production: Florida grapefruits account for well over half the worldwide output of the fruit. Florida grapefruit can be found in the Orient, in Europe, and just about anywhere else there is a taste for citrus. Giving fuel to the Florida growers' case that they have the best grapefruit is the state's crown jewel, the ***Marsh White,*** one of the world's best grapefruits, if not *the* best. In fact, it's the only commercially grown light-fleshed grapefruit. The skin is a nice, smooth yellow with medium thickness, making it easy to peel (also true of the ***Texas Ruby***), and it's juicy and nearly seedless.

Both Texas and Florida have famous growing areas. In the Lone Star state, it's the Rio Grande Valley near Mexico. Florida's pride is the Indian River region. Between Daytona in the north and Palm Beach in the South, this area is perfect for citrus growing. Now within Indian River is an area named Orchid Island, and every piece of fruit shipped from that area bears a label saying Orchid or Orchid Island. This is the sign of the world's best, and the price tag matches the quality. Remember, the Gulf Stream is out in the Atlantic, so warm temperatures protect the groves at night when the mildest frost could wipe out an entire industry. (Maybe I shouldn't talk about frost; the Texas crop was destroyed by frost during the early part of the 1980s and has just gotten back on track during the past few years.)

When shopping for grapefruit, choose heavy fruit of uniform size. Don't bother about rough skin or skin color, for it's the weight that tells you whether it's nice and juicy. Grapefruit are available year-round, with Florida producing them September through July; Texas, October through July; California, October through February; and Arizona, October through summer. The grapefruit is not quite as nutritious as the other citrus fruits, but it does contain small amounts of vitamins A and B and fair amounts of vitamin C, and it is low in calories.

Grapes

AVAILABLE
year-round

DOMESTIC PEAK
late May-January

The grape was introduced to California by Spanish padres as they opened missions throughout the west. However, by no means was this the first introduction of the fruit to America. In fact, hundreds of years before Columbus found America, the Viking sailors crossed the Great North Sea and visited what is now the New England coastline. They were amazed to see the abundance of native grapevines, so they called the area "Vinland."

The grape is believed to be the first fruit cultivated by human beings, an association that is well documented throughout the Bible. According to the book of Genesis, one of the first things that Noah did after the Flood was to plant a vineyard. The grape has been around so long and seems to be native to so many lands that its exact origin remains unknown.

There are literally hundreds of varieties of this ancient fruit: two native American grapes are the **Northern Fox** and the **Muscadine** (this one is still enjoyed in the southern United States). These are considered the parents of today's commercially grown native grapes: the **Niagara,** the **Delaware,** and the most popular of the domestic grapes, the **Concord.** These varieties, for the most part, are used for eating out of hand. They have thick skins and seeds.

The vineyards planted by the padres are direct descendants of the Old World grapes described in the Bible. They have thinner skins and an overall sweeter flavor. Some of today's table grapes include the **Perlette,** a small green seedless grape with a somewhat thick skin. It grows in a tight cluster and has a nice sweet flavor.

The grape is believed to be the first fruit cultivated.

Today's most popular grape is the **Thompson Seedless.** This large, green grape is sometimes as long as one inch. When you see this seedless grape with a rich yellow color, that indicates the sugar levels are at their highest.

Another grape is the **Flame Seedless.** Many think this red seedless will surpass the Thompson in popularity, but I don't think so. It has beautiful color and a wonderful sweet flavor, but it's just not as juicy as the Thompson.

If any grape can become more popular than the Thompson, I think it will be the **Exotic.** The Exotic is a black seedless grape that is a little smaller than the Thompson, but it is just as sweet and juicy. As soon as farmers catch on, watch out, Thompson! This grape adds beauty to any fruit arrangement.

The forerunner to the Exotic is the **Ribier.** This black grape is surpassed by none as far as flavor is concerned, but most consumers want seedless grapes, and the Ribier has three large pits.

There are many other grapes you should also try. For instance, the **Queen** is a red grape that is sweet, firm, and crisp to bite. The **Tokay** is sure to be a hit in the nineties—it's the red counterpart to the Perlette. The **Italia** is large, sweet, and juicy, with a muscat flavor. Another grape that should become quite popular in the next few years is the **Black Corinth,** more commonly known as the "Champagne Grape" because of its tiny size, like the bubbles of its namesake. The flavor is outstanding.

Grapes are available year-round. Domestic crops start in late May and wind down in January. During the off months, the bulk of the imports comes in from Chile, with a smaller amount arriving from Mexico. When shopping for grapes, remember that freshness is key: the fruit should cling firmly to the stem; it should not shake loose easily. The stem should be green with no indication of drying, which is a sign of age. The fruit will keep up to a week in your refrigerator, but should be consumed within three days if possible.

Grapes aren't known for their nutritional value, but they do contain some of vitamins A and C.

Guavas

AVAILABLE
mid-July-
October

Those who have tried Hawaiian guavas say that no others can compare. Unfortunately, Hawaiian guavas aren't sold on the mainland, and I'm sure you would like to know the reason that this tropical gift can't be found in your local market. Our youngest state happens to be one of the most popular breeding grounds for the fruit fly, and the attractive guava is an ideal host to that dreadful pest, so this exotic fruit cannot be exported to the mainland unless it has been fumigated. Due to the fragility of the tree-ripened Hawaiian guava, unlike other Hawaiian fruits, it cannot withstand the fumigation process; as a result, we consumers miss the opportunity to have this fruit on a regular basis.

The origin of the guava is not clear. Some believe it originated in Mexico; other sources say the Caribbean. The guava you are most likely to find in your local market comes from south Florida.

The fruit color is light green or yellow, and the size is that of a golfball. The tree-ripened ones I tried were wonderful, and they weren't from Hawaii. Guava tastes sweet, almost strawberry-like, and smells like a beautiful flower. The seeds are also edible.

Choose firm, bruise-free guavas that have a slight give at the blossom end. The ripe fruit has one of the most pleasant smells in nature. Firm guavas will store unrefrigerated for two or three days; after the fruit has softened it should be refrigerated.

Like most tropical fruit, the guava is high in vitamin C and low in calories. The season spans from middle to late July through October.

Kiwi-fruit

The kiwi originated in China, where it was known as Yang Tao. During the early part of the twentieth century, the kiwi made its way to New Zealand, where it thrived and was renamed Chinese Gooseberry. Another name change was in store for the ancient Yang Tao. In 1960, New Zealand businessmen called it kiwi-fruit when marketing it in the United States. The name was taken from the kiwi bird native to New Zealand, which is little, brown, and fuzzy, like the fruit. Those New Zealanders did such a good job marketing the kiwi-fruit that most people think it is native to New Zealand.

During the 1960s, the kiwi crop was introduced to Southern California and has since become a major cash crop. Shoppers are lucky, because with New Zealand being in the southern hemisphere and California in the northern hemisphere, reverse growing seasons make kiwi available year-round. California kiwi is in season November through late May; New Zealand kiwi, May through December.

AVAILABLE
year-round

DOMESTIC PEAK
November-late May

As for taste, the kiwi is fantastic—sweet and tangy. The flesh color is lime green with hundreds of tiny, edible black seeds. Biting into a sweet kiwi, you might think it is loaded with calories. Wrong! The average kiwi contains only about thirty calories and more than half the daily requirement of vitamin C.

Like papaya, kiwi is a natural meat tenderizer.

Kiwi is wonderful in cooking; it is a natural meat tenderizer, like papaya. Rub it into beef steak before cooking. I love to marinate chicken in kiwi, white wine, and a bit of salt and pepper. The chicken is great grilled or baked. Another way to enjoy this Asian delight is with cream. And kiwi juice added to iced tea is refreshing.

When shopping, choose firm, unbruised fruit and allow it to ripen at room temperature for two to three days. When the fruit is ripe, it will keep four to five additional days in the refrigerator.

CITY AND COUNTRY KIWI DESSERT

6 peaches, peeled
and sliced
4 kiwi, peeled
and sliced
1 cup fresh orange
juice
4 oz. wine

Place all ingredients in a large bowl. Cover and chill about 8 hours before serving. Excellent alone or over vanilla ice cream.

Lemons

Can you believe it? From one of the most sour fruits comes one of our favorite liquid refreshments—lemonade.

AVAILABLE
year-round

The lemon, like all the members of the citrus family, originated in Asia and today is grown in virtually every warm climate zone on earth. The U.S. is the leading producer of lemons, with California, Arizona, and Florida being the leading domestic producers.

The California growers came of age during the Gold Rush of

the mid-1800s. In the California gold country, fresh fruits—and vegetables, for that matter—were hard to come by. The production of lemons was increased to help in the fight against scurvy, a disease caused when the body lacks vitamin C. Scurvy results in weakness, anemia, soft gums, and bleeding, and it could be fatal. Today lemons sell for as little as five cents sometimes, but during the scurvy-ridden days of the 1800s that same lemon would fetch prices well over one dollar. Hard to imagine.

There are many varieties of lemons, but I'm only going to mention two because they are the major sellers. First is the ***Eureka.*** It has plenty of juice that is quite acidic, with very few seeds. This variety has the shape and size of the fresh, double-yolk eggs I gathered as a little boy at my grandmama's and granddad's house in north Georgia. The skin seems thick and bumpy, with many of what I call inward freckles. The stem end is quite flat and the color is rainbow yellow.

The other variety is the ***Lisbon.*** It, too, provides plenty of juice and has several seeds. The skin is much smoother, with a longer stem end.

Now that I've walked you down the varietal path, I'm going to tell you not to concern yourself with varieties, because lemons are only sold as—um—lemons. The grade of lemons is based on clearness, texture, and skin color, not largeness. If lemons are too big, they tend to become dry, and the skin is tough. Often lemons don't receive top grades because they have cuts or bruises. Again, don't worry about grades of lemons because they are based on the outside, not the juice content. So don't pay attention to grading unless you need beautiful lemon rinds.

As for availability, if you walk into a lemon grove, be it winter, spring, summer, or fall, you will see three things on the trees: flowers, buds, and fruit. The trees are ever-bearing, making lemons in season year-round. The Eureka reaches its peak output during summer, whereas the Lisbon peaks during winter.

When shopping for lemons, look for color first; it should be a rich yellow—that rainbow yellow I mentioned earlier. Remember that with age, that yellow dulls. It's okay if a bit of light green is present around the stem, as this is a sign of freshness. Choose fruit about 3 to maybe 3-1/2 inches long—if it's longer than that, it starts to toughen up. Now, the most important key: as with all citrus, the lemon should be heavy for its size; that lets you know the fruit you selected is full of juice. One more thing: as with all citrus, normally the thinner the skin, the juicier the fruit.

Lemons will keep for weeks in the refrigerator. However, I suggest you use them within a week. If you can't do that, then squeeze the juice into a bottle and freeze the rind until needed.

We all know that lemon is loaded with vitamin C. It also contains protein, calcium, carbohydrates, iron, and phosphorus, and it's low in calories.

When I want to keep my calories down, the only salad dressing I use is lemon juice mixed with mustard and a bit of salt and pepper. Try it, keeping in mind that you can also add fresh herbs.

Limes

AVAILABLE
year-round

I must be honest with you—this is a fruit I hardly ever use. I can't really tell you why, because the few times a year I eat them, be it at a Mexican restaurant or in a friend's guacamole, I enjoy the taste, and when I get down to south Florida, I love Key Lime pie. I just don't think to use limes in my recipes. So, no matter what I say from this point on, keep in mind that limes can be used any place lemons are.

Earlier I told you about the lemon and how it was used in the fight against scurvy in California's gold country. Well, limes, too, have a place in world history in the war against that disease. Over two centuries ago the British navy had trouble with scurvy on long trips (no wonder, with the majority of meals after the first week or so consisting of stale bread and sour meat), so on a daily basis the seamen would receive allowances of lime. By the way, that's why British sailors are called limeys—no joke.

As with lemons, there are many varieties of limes, but don't worry about varieties because you won't see them listed in your retail store—with the possible exception of *Key Limes.* This is the same type imported from Mexico during the domestic off-season. The Key or Mexican lime is oval-shaped with thin, leather-like skin that is a yellow-green color.

The texture and flavor are quite similar in limes and lemons. I guess the biggest difference between the two, other than color, is smell. Fresh limes have an almost flower-like fragrance.

Like lemons, limes are available year-round, with the domestic season peaking during summer, when the fruit offers the best flavor and the lowest prices. In other countries the lime is used often in cooked dishes: seafoods, meats, and vegetarian meals; whereas at home we most often use the lime to flavor liquid refreshments. However, that is slowly starting to change.

When shopping, remember that the greener the skin, the fresher the lime. Again, choose fruit that is heavy for its size. Yellowing in the skin is a sign of age, and the juice will lack acid. Don't be too concerned about a few dark spots; however, avoid fruit that has dry, shriveled skin with black spots.

Lime will keep for weeks under refrigeration, but again, I suggest you use them within a few days for best flavor and nutritional value. Sunlight causes the skin color to fade to a pale yellow, draining the fruit juice of its acid. So as soon as you get them, put them in the refrigerator.

The nutritional value of the lime is quite good. It contains plenty of vitamin C and good amounts of protein, calcium, and iron. Limes are low in fat and calories.

Mangoes

AVAILABLE

year-round

DOMESTIC

PEAK

winter

Until recently, the mango was considered exotic here in the U.S. In the tropical parts of the world, the mango is as popular as the Red Delicious apple is in Washington State. In fact, in the tropics they say the mango is the forbidden fruit because it's so sweet, it must be sinful to eat. The mango is believed to have originated in India, and it has been cultivated for over four thousand years. Settlers brought it to America in the 1700s.

This fruit of an evergreen tree now grows in tropical regions throughout the world. The tree is considered the pride of the garden. The taste of its delicate fruit, very attractive in appearance, is difficult to describe. Some say it tastes like a cross between a pineapple and a melon.

Most of the mangoes seen in the market are about the size of a large avocado, but may weigh as much as three pounds, with colors that range from green to bright yellow to gold to pink to clear red. A blend of several colors is often evident on the ripening fruit.

Since they're grown in the tropics, mangoes are available in the U.S. markets year-round. They're at their peak during our winter.

When shopping, look for smooth-skinned mangoes that have started to show color. A firm mango with some "give" is ready to eat. Truly green ones may never ripen, but are good for cooking. (Try making a mango soup with green mangoes; let me know what you think.) Fruit that is shriveled and has black spots is overripe, so don't select those.

One-half of a mango has only about sixty-five calories and will supply half of an adult's daily requirement of vitamin C. Mangoes are also high in vitamin A.

Mangoes can be very juicy and messy to eat. You might want to eat them over the sink.

Melons

My all-time favorite melon is the **Crane Melon,** a product of the cross-pollination of at least three melons. The skin is smooth and cream-colored, like that of the honeydew melon. When ripe, the skin color changes to a light orange. The melon smells tropically sweet, with a tangy sweet flavor, and its inside is a deep sunset-orange color.

Another nice choice is the **Cranshaw,** the third highest selling melon in America. This melon has yellow skin and gold flesh. When ripe, it is the sweetest and juiciest of all melons. I think the Cranshaw tastes best when ice-cold. Its season runs August through December.

The next melon I recommend is the **Persian,** but it has a very short season—August to early October. When ripe, it looks like a super-sized cantaloupe. Never buy Persian melons that are green in color; they are not ripe and will never reach their peak flavor. When you pick a Persian with that light orange color, you are in for a special treat.

Now, if you really need a change, ask your greengrocer for a **Sharlyn** melon, though it might be hard to get because it's fairly new. The Sharlyn has white flesh, which makes it stand out in fruit salads, and its flavor allows it to stand alone. It's sweet like the Cranshaw, but not as juicy.

If it's winter and you want a melon grown in America, what do you do? Ask for the **Santa Claus.** It looks like a big green football with stripes—long on looks, but short on flavor.

I also recommend the **Galia** melon during winter. The best are flown in from Israel, which makes them costly, but it's worth more to have a sweet and juicy melon like this for Christmas. In recent years, growers in Latin America and Puerto Rico have begun to ship the Galia to the United States. They taste good, but the best are still from Israel.

AVAILABLE *varieties, year-round*

DOMESTIC PEAK *June-November*

Most experts say there are three keys to picking ripe melons: sight, touch, and smell. I think there is a fourth: buying melons in season. Cantaloupe and honeydew are available year-round, peaking June through November; Honeyloupe, a cross of the two melons, is available August through November; Cranshaw, Persian, and Sharlyn, August through October; and Santa Claus, November through February. Remember that most melons peak around midseason.

Choose an even-colored melon with no sign of mold that is firm around the middle and has some give at the blossom end. Immature melons have little or no odor; when ripe they are as fragrant as a flowerbed.

Uncut melons will keep three to four days unrefrigerated and up to a week refrigerated. Eat within two days after cutting.

Melons are a good source for vitamins A and C and protein, yet are low in calories.

MELON SOUP

8 lbs. melons
  (*your choice*)
2 tsp. vegetable oil
2 fresh chili peppers,
  seeded and
  chopped
1/2 cup white wine
2/3 cup lemon juice
2 Tbl. honey
1/4 tsp. pepper

Cut melons, remove seeds, and scoop out flesh; set aside. In a saucepan, heat oil. Cook peppers about 4 minutes. Add wine and boil. In a large bowl, mix melons with hot wine and peppers. Add other ingredients. Purée in blender. Chill before serving.

Cantaloupe

The nation's favorite melon is available year-round, with the domestic season peaking July through mid- to late-September. However, most years there are excellent domestic 'lopes (as we call them in the wholesale business) on the market up until November.

AVAILABLE
year-round

When shopping for cantaloupe, the first thing you need to do is pick the melon up and turn it back and forth near your ear. If you hear a sloshing sound, pass on that piece of fruit, for that sound is a sign of age or improper storage. The sloshing sound tells you that the membrane that holds the seed cluster to the flesh has given way because of age or heat. Be sure to perform this test with any melon you intend to purchase.

DOMESTIC PEAK
July-late September

After the fruit passes the slosh test, check its color. What you are looking for is a light tan color. You want that color from stem end to blossom end (the stem end is where the melon was cut from the vine). If the netting of the melon shows any green, that is a sign of immaturity, and the fruit may never reach a sweet, juicy flavor. Last, put your nose to work at the blossom end of the melon. When ripe, the cantaloupe gives off a sweet, flower-like smell. The melon should yield slightly at the blossom end.

I try to buy melons the day I want to serve them. However, firm, ripe cantaloupes will keep two to three days at room temperature, or up to a week under refrigeration.

Cantaloupe is a great source of vitamin A. It contains a fair amount of vitamin C, calcium, and iron.

Honeydew

AVAILABLE
*late May-
late September*

**DOMESTIC
PEAK**
July-August

I have a funny relationship with this melon. Normally, I don't think much of it and don't recommend it to retail shoppers. I would say I don't like it—unless you happen to catch me while eating, or just having finished, a vine-ripened slice. In those moments the honeydew is nature's most wonderful and delightful gift, and for the life of me I can't explain why that feeling doesn't last. So when I start talking about shopping, please put my advice to work in your local produce section.

Honeydew, like its cousin, cantaloupe, is available pretty much year-round. The domestic season begins in late May or early June and winds down in September or October. Peak flavor and lowest prices are usually found in July and August.

When you're shopping, a ripe honeydew calls out to you with its rose-like fragrance; let your nose enjoy what your taste buds will later. If no fragrance is present, no flavor will be either.

After assessing the fruit's aroma, try the slosh test I told you about in the cantaloupe section. Then look at the color. Some describe the rind of a ripe honeydew as a creamy, butter-like pale yellow. I think that description works. You want to see good color from the stem to the blossom end; if the background of the melon shows green, chances are it will never reach the wonderful sweetness we all love. The "dew" should be firm, but should give to pressure around the middle and at the blossom end. In the produce market, be patient and shop carefully, as most of the time we're talking about a two- to four-dollar investment.

Try to purchase the melon the day you want to serve it. However, it will keep a day or two at room temperature if it's firm-ripe. In the refrigerator the melon is okay for at least a week.

There is another storage tip for all melons, including water-melon. It took me years to accept this, but my sister Laura Regina made me a believer: the day you buy the fresh, ripe melon, slice it into plastic containers, burp them, and the fruit will last up to ten days, sometimes longer.

The honeydew contains a fair amount of vitamins A and C. It's low in calories and provides some protein and calcium.

Pepinos

The pepino is one of the most exciting newcomers to the world of exotic and fancy fruits. The pepino is a melon, although to look at it you would never guess. It is shaped like a miniature football, three to six inches long. The skin is purple with yellowish stripes. The flesh is the part that reveals its melon secret. The texture and flavor remind me of a ripe cantaloupe or honeydew. Its color is a yellowish-orange that is quite pleasing to the eye and makes a wonderful addition to fruit salad.

AVAILABLE
*January-
mid-summer*

The pepino, a native of South America, is high in potassium as well as vitamin C. Although most pepinos sold in America come from New Zealand, California has begun to produce the fruit as a cash crop.

The pepino is available starting in late January, running through mid-summer. As for selecting a pepino, most fruit sold in retail stores in the United States is still quite green, so be sure to choose fruit without scars or bruises, and allow it to ripen at room temperature or until the skin shows that yellow tint and becomes softer. The pepino also has a nice fruity fragrance when ripe.

Watermelons

AVAILABLE
year-round

**DOMESTIC
PEAK**
*April-
November*

It is hard to believe that the watermelon is a member of the same botanical family as squash and cucumbers, but it is. This edible gourd originated in Africa. The early African tribesmen would carry watermelons as a source of moisture on long hunting trips, when fresh water would be hard to come by. This melon was brought to America by the early European settlers and, as it did in its homeland of Africa and on the contintent of Europe, watermelon rather quickly became a favorite throughout the thirteen colonies. Watermelons are now grown in more than half of the continental United States. California leads the way in production; however, the southern states lead the way when it comes to taste, and heading up that group is my home state of Georgia, which I believe produces the sweetest, juiciest watermelons in the country.

There are many watermelon varieties, and they come in all shapes, sizes, and colors. The flesh color can be red or yellow, and over the past few years, I have seen orange flesh. I should point out that the latter two can be, and often are, just as sweet as the red-fleshed watermelon. However, red watermelon outsells the yellow and orange varieties by at least eight to one.

Here are some of the more popular varieties: out west, the solid green **Peacock** has been a long time favorite, but one of the southern favorites, the oval-shaped, pale green **Charleston Gray,** is quickly gaining popularity. In the South and on the East Coast, along with the Charleston Gray, other excellent watermelons include the **Crimson Sweet,** another pale green melon, and the **Jubilee,** a light green variety with dark green stripes (this one has a flesh color that is fire-engine red and is very sweet). My favorite is the **Black Diamond;** the best of these come from Franklin County, Georgia. The Diamond is round or somewhat oval with a skin color so dark and green that it looks black. Inside, the rind is snow-white and the meat is a beautiful red, not as rich in color as the Jubilee, but equally pretty and, oh, so sweet.

In Canada, the so-called ***icebox*** melons are preferred. These are the smaller versions of watermelons, weighing from two to ten pounds. Leading that pack is the sweet little ***Sugar Baby*** melon, a miniature version of the Black Diamond.

Watermelons are available year-round, but if you are like me and prefer the domestic varieties, you'll find them on the market from late April through November. At other times of the year, they come up from Mexico and Central America.

How to select a good watermelon? Most of us who have been in this business a little while try to sidestep the question because it is hit-or-miss when it comes to picking a good watermelon. You can thump and slap as much as you want and still pick a bad watermelon. When the real pros, the growers, think a field is ripe and ready to be picked, they cut ten to fifteen melons just to see if the taste and color are ready. So the only way to tell if you have really picked a good melon is to cut it and try it.

As for nutrition, watermelons are quite low in calories, and are an excellent source of potassium. They also provide a fair amount of vitamin A and calcium.

Nectarines

AVAILABLE

*June-
September*

Nectarines, like their distant cousins, peaches, originated centuries ago in China and made their way west along ancient trade routes. One country along that route was Greece, where the fruit was so popular its juice was called the "drink of the gods." The Greek word for that is *nektar,* thus the name nectarine. Here in the United States, nectarines have always been popular in the areas where they are grown, but until 1940 the fruit had one major drawback. When ripe, it was very soft and delicate. It could not withstand the torture of shipment, so nectarines remained a very localized fruit, until the development of the first gold-fleshed freestone (the flesh does not adhere to the seed) variety in La Grande, California (about 90 years after the first freestone peach was developed). Like that first peach, the Elberta, the first nectarine, **La Grande,** is still in production.

Since the development of the La Grande, a hybrid nectarine that is able to withstand the punishment of shipment, the nectarine has enjoyed increasing popularity throughout America and the world. Since 1940, over one hundred new varieties of nectarines have been introduced; however, out of all the different nectarines grown in the United States, twelve make up the bulk of the fruit sold to retail consumers: **May Grand, Early Sun Grand, Fire Bright, Spring Red, Red Diamond, Flavor Top, Summer Grand, Fiesta, Royal Giant, Red Gem, Flame-Kist,** and **Red Gold.**

Selecting nectarines is pretty much like selecting peaches. Choose hard fruit, for they will ripen at room temperature, but avoid fruit that still shows green in the color of the skin. Like peaches, nectarines are an excellent source for vitamin A; however, they are a bit higher in calories than other soft fruits. The seasons are similar to the seasons for peaches: June through September.

Oranges

The best oranges are grown in the western hemisphere, although *Jaffa* (Israeli navel oranges) are quite good. There are many varieties; however, two stand out for me. My favorite, *Valencia* (best for fresh orange juice), is the pineapple orange. This little, round, beautiful orange is sweet and juicy; it has a lot of seeds, but that's okay if you like good taste. The name comes from the sweet smell.

AVAILABLE
year-round

The best oranges for eating out of hand are the navels. The Florida navels are big, sweet, and very juicy. The peels aren't quite as thick as their West Coast counterpart, due to Florida's hot days and warm nights, which sometimes keep the peel from becoming completely orange. It's okay to buy Florida oranges that show green in the peel. They will still be sweet and juicy. The California navel has a thick skin, which makes it very easy to peel, and the segments are much easier to divide. The orange color of the West Coast navel is very deep when compared to Florida's crop, and they're not as juicy (but are just as sweet). My favorite navel orange is the *Washington Navel.* No, they are not grown in Washington State. This orange came to America by way of Brazil. Missionaries sent the Department of Agriculture several trees in the mid-1800s. The offspring of those trees still thrive today in California.

**DOMESTIC
PEAK**
*November-
April*

Remember, oranges are available year-round, but the highest volume and best quality can be found from November through April and sometimes into May. Don't concern yourself with the color so much as the weight of the orange, and make sure the skin has not dried out. Oranges are loaded with vitamin C.

Papaya

Even though it's an American native, the papaya was considered strange and exotic here until the mid-twentieth century. This pear-shaped delight is believed to have originated in Central or South America. It rapidly spread throughout the tropical region.

The first time I saw a papaya dangling from a tree was in the summer of '88 in Key West, Florida. I was visiting the historical site that was once the home of Ernest Hemingway. To the left of the main house is a garden cut out of the coral reef on which Key West sits. In that garden was a papaw (sometimes spelled pawpaw) tree that stood twenty feet tall, dark green in color from the stalk to the tip of its leaves. It was an absolutely beautiful plant. The fruit of the papaw tree is the papaya, and this one was dangling from what looked like long green ropes. I had to restrain myself from plucking that papaya from Papa Hemingway's tree.

In the American tropics, many varieties still grow in the wild. Some are less than two inches long and weigh just ounces; others grow to be as large as volleyballs, weighing pounds. It wasn't until the 1800s that the papaya was introduced to its ideal tropical region, Hawaii, which is by far the largest supplier of fresh papaya to the mainland United States.

The variety most often cultivated in Hawaii is the **Solo.** Unlike the wild varieties, the Solo grows more uniformly, is six to eight inches long, and weighs about one to two pounds, which makes it perfect for packing and shipping. The Solo is a beautiful yellow variety that is extremely sweet and juicy.

There is another variety grown in Hawaii that unfortunately is not available to the mainland consumer. It is the **Sunrise,** which is even sweeter than the Solo and has more of a reddish-orange color. I think the American consumer would absolutely love the Sunrise papaya. However, like other delicate tropical fruits, the

Sunrise papaya can't withstand the fumigation process required before shipment to the mainland.

The papaya is truly one of nature's wonderful gifts. In addition to its exquisite flavor, it is a natural meat tenderizer, which makes it excellent for cooking.

Selecting papaya is simple. The fruit ripens from bottom to top, or blossom end to stem. Its color changes from green to sunshine yellow, much like a banana, and as its color changes, the sugar content rises. I have found that when about one-fourth of the papaya has turned yellow, its sugar content is high enough for the fruit to be quite tasty. Also, at that point, it is perfect to cook with.

After the papaya has fully ripened, it can be stored in the refrigerator for two or three days. There are very few fruits that are as naturally sweet as the papaya, yet remain as low in calories (about thirty-nine per serving). It is an excellent source for vitamins A, B, and C, and it also contains large amounts of phosphorus and potassium. Here are two good papaya recipes:

First, a papaya sauce that is excellent over vegetables or meat dishes.

Papaya Sauce

In a saucepan, combine all ingredients. Bring to a simmer. Pour into blender. Purée. Return mixture to saucepan. Simmer again. Serve over chicken or vegetables.

half a papaya, peeled, seeded, and sliced
dash of salt and pepper
1 tsp. lemon juice

Papaya Roasted Chicken

In a roasting pan, place one layer of diced papaya. Place chicken on top of papaya. Smother with remaining ingredients. Roast in preheated 325 degree oven 45 minutes (longer if needed).

1 chicken, cut up
1 papaya, peeled, seeded, and diced
half a green pepper
half an onion, diced
Salt and pepper to taste

Passion Fruit

AVAILABLE
*March-
September*

Like the cherimoya, the Passion Fruit is native to South America. The fruits have other similarities as well. Both thrive in subtropical and tropical regions of the world, and when they are ripe, they have very unusual appearances.

The common name, Passion Fruit, does not come from the fruit's ability to stimulate romantic endeavors, although most retailers would lead you to believe that. The truth is quite the opposite.

Until quite recently, the ***granadilla*** or Passion Plant was cultivated for its ornamental value—to be more specific, its flower. The early Christian missionaries in South America are believed to have renamed this flower "Passion Flower" after observing similarities between the flower's inner petals and the crown of thorns placed on the head of Jesus Christ, and other symbols of the crucifixion. So the name is really in remembrance of the passion of Christ.

My first encounter with Passion Fruit came during my second week at Peaches Produce in San Francisco. A customer ordered a case, and I was so disappointed when I delivered this box of wrinkled fruit that had some mold on it. I promised my customer that the next case would be perfect; he looked at me and laughed long and hard. He finally said, "Curtis, these *are* perfect. That's what the fruit looks like when it is ripe."

The taste is very exotic (sweet, with a little tartness), and the smell is truly heavenly. The season runs from March through September. To select, choose fruit high in color: in the New Zealand variety, purple; in the Hawaiian, a little lighter in color. If the shell (or skin) is smooth and hard, allow the fruit time to ripen at room temperature. You will know it is ready to eat when the fruit has wrinkled and shriveled and the shell has become much softer.

As for nutrition, although Passion Fruit is quite sweet and provides some vitamin C, it remains very low in calories—about fifteen per fruit.

Peaches

Many areas of the world are proud producers of this ancient fruit. During winter, Chile and Australia are among the countries that ship fresh peaches to the United States, and at home, states fight to lay claim to the various peach honors. Arizona and California bicker each year about which state will produce the first peach of the domestic season. New Jersey and Pennsylvania argue over which state produces the best peach north of the Mason-Dixon line. In the South, South Carolina lays claim to number one in peach production, but no state dares to claim that it produces a better peach than Georgia.

AVAILABLE
year-round

DOMESTIC PEAK
mid-June-August

How did the Chinese symbol of long life become a proud product of American agriculture? In 1850, the Rumphy family of Georgia received peach buddings from China. The trees grew and produced like crazy. Supposedly, Mrs. Rumphy dropped several pits into a basket and forgot about them until years later when her grandson started his orchard. He planted the pits and this cling-type (the flesh adheres to the seed) peach tree grew and bloomed. Cross-pollination took place between the new trees and older ones. The end result of this fluke of nature was a golden freestone (the seed is loose inside the fruit) variety, which young Rumphy named Elberta, after his wife. The Elberta is worlds apart from the small, hard, and sour peach that originated in China centuries before the birth of Christ.

The ***Elberta*** peach—descendant of the cling variety, and considered forebear of all the freestone peaches—was once so popular that it alone accounted for over 90 percent of the total peach sales in the United States. Today, that percentage has dropped to about 50 percent. If you are still not clear about cling and freestone peaches, maybe this will help. If you took a cling peach and tried to slice it in half, flesh would adhere to the seed. Do the same to a freestone, and the seed would pop right out.

As popular as the Elberta was, and still is, there are many other great tasting peaches you may want to look for and try. Here are a few. Among white peaches, try the early **Babcock** and a Southern favorite, **Georgia Belle.** As for the yellow and red flesh, try the ladies: **June Lady** and **Elegant Lady.** Both have attractive red skin and beautiful golden flesh with tints of red. Other national favorites are **O-Henry, Red Haven,** and the **Fay Elberta.**

When selecting fresh peaches, it is fine to choose hard fruit because it will ripen at room temperature and it is good for cooking. However, avoid peaches that still show green in the color of the skin. Those peaches were harvested too soon and usually dry out before ripening completely. Now, the key to choosing sweet and juicy peaches is at the end of your face. Don't be afraid to follow your nose. If it smells peachy, then it tastes peachy. The season begins in May and peaks mid-June through August. The entire season winds down in September. You can find domestic peaches available in October, but I recommend avoiding them because they have been in storage for quite some time.

The peach is a great source of vitamin A and is relatively low in calories—a medium peach usually contains about fifty.

Pears

The pear is a member of the rose family, like the apple and quince. There are hundreds of varieties of pears in existence, but only a dozen or so are grown commercially.

My favorite pear is a perfect example of the saying, "beauty is only skin deep." The **Comice** is ugly, but beneath that peel is the most flavorful, sweet, and juicy pear in the world. In Europe, this pear is such a prize that shoppers begin to anticipate its arrival a month before the season begins, and in some restaurants it is served alone as a dessert. Its season is October and November, but it's still available from storage through the winter.

The next pear, if it were entered in a beauty contest, would take first prize hands down. The **Bosc** is the most shapely of pears, and when ripe it has a dark tan color. This pear is not very juicy, but it is quite sweet and has a nutty flavor. I think the Bosc is best when still very firm and crunchy. They're available October through May.

The next two pears are primarily used as decorations. The **Forelle,** most experts say, is long on looks and short on flavor, but I think they are very wrong. When ripe, this shapely, freckled miniature pear is sweet and still crisp when you buy it. Sometimes, though, you will run into a tart Forelle. Don't let that discourage you from buying it; this pear is great on a cheese platter.

Most pears were introduced to this country from Europe and other parts of the world, but the **Seckel** pear is a North American native. It was discovered in Pennsylvania in the early 1800s near the Delaware River. This is the smallest of all varieties of pears; it is not much larger than a golf ball. When ripe, it is dull green with red cheeks. The Seckel pear is an eastern pear, but the best are grown out west in California, Oregon, and Washington. This is a sweet and juicy little pear whose season runs September through January.

AVAILABLE
year-round

DOMESTIC PEAK
August-January

The pear is a member of the rose family, like the apple and quince.

The **Williams** pear, more commonly known in America as the **Bartlett,** is the world's best-selling pear. It is the first pear of the season starting in late summer and is available well into fall. Over the past few years, a red variety of Bartlett has been gaining popularity. It's not quite as sweet as its more familiar yellow relative, but does possess outstanding flavor.

The most popular winter pear is the **Anjou.** It was introduced to America during the mid-1800s. The Anjou looks similar to the Bartlett but has a shorter top and when ripe is not quite as yellow.

Pears are available year-round, but with most of the domestic varieties, the season runs late summer through late winter. You should select firm, unscarred fruit, and allow it to ripen at room temperature. You can tell pears are ripe when you press against the stem end and there is a slight give. There is an exception to every rule, and the Bosc pear,which is best when still very firm, is the one exception to this rule.

Out of all the deciduous fruits, pears have the highest calorie (ninety) and sugar counts. However, they are also loaded with carbohydrates, calcium, and potassium.

FRUIT & SORBET DELIGHT

1 Comice pear, halved
1 cup of assorted berries
berry sorbet *(see recipe below)*

Slice any large berries and arrange 3/4 of them in a bed in a dish. Peel and core the Comice pear and place on top of the berry bed. Place the remaining sliced berries inside the pear, then pour the berry sorbet over the top.

BERRY SORBET

1 cup favorite berries
honey to taste

Purée berries with honey. Heat if desired.

Persimmons

The persimmon is an autumn fruit, like the pomegranate. When I was growing up, there was a pretty little tree with large berries on it in our backyard. Later I found out they were not berries at all; they were persimmons (not the big, shapely varieties you find in gourmet stores today, but the smaller, less attractive ones that are native to North America, the Southern states in particular). If you have ever bitten into an unripe persimmon, you know why my childhood memories of it are sour. It is like biting into a very unripe lime. It just locks your mouth up. No matter how much water you drink, it stays dry. Everyone would tell me, "You just have to pick them when they're ripe; they are so sweet and juicy." Well, finally I gave up on trying to pick a ripe persimmon, until a few years ago when shopping in New York City's Hunt's Point Market. An old-timer was eating a ripe persimmon and seemed to be truly enjoying it. He taught me the secret to selecting and ripening persimmons.

I remember telling him, "I have never met a persimmon I liked or one that liked me. They always make my mouth feel like the Sahara Desert." He replied, "You just didn't know what you were buying." Then he said, "Pick yourself a nice, pretty piece of fruit and let it sit until it wrinkles up and becomes nice and soft." I jumped in and said, "Yeah, then is it ripe?" "No," he said, "wait two more days. Then it's ripe." He was right. When ripe, very few fruits can match persimmons for sweetness, and they are so soft and juicy.

The wild persimmons that grew in my backyard when I was a child had very little in common with the persimmons you will find in the retail stores of today. This fruit is native to Asia and is still very popular in that part of the world. The persimmon is like no other fruit; however, the persimmon tree is related to the ebony tree. Ebony wood is used in making expensive furniture, and persimmon wood is used in the manufacturing of wooden golf club heads. You know, some say the growing popularity of golf is the reason the

AVAILABLE
October-January

*You can take
an unripe
persimmon,
freeze it
overnight, and
when it thaws
out it will be
completely
ripe and
sweet.*

acreage of persimmon trees has dropped in recent decades. I wonder, now that metal "woods" have been introduced to golf, if more persimmon trees will be allowed to mature and bear fruit.

There are many varieties of persimmons; however, only two varieties are grown and packed for sale in California, which provides all the United States' commercial crops. The first is **Hachiya,** which makes up over 80 percent of all persimmons sold annually in the United States. It is just beautiful to look at. It is shaped like an acorn, but is much larger, about the size of a nectarine, sometimes weighing as much as a pound and a half. The color is orange, bright, and shiny. Warning! Never bite into the Hachiya persimmon until it is fully ripe because it will lock up your mouth. To be sure a persimmon is ripe, allow it to soften until the skin wrinkles and it is soft to touch.

The **Fuyu** is the other commercially grown variety. It's not too big and not very pretty. This variety looks like a dull orange tomato. Fuyus is not as sweet as the Hachiya, but does have one good thing going: it can be eaten while still firm and not dry your mouth out.

You can take an unripe persimmon, freeze it overnight, and when it thaws out it will be completely ripe and sweet. As for nutrition, persimmons have a fair amount of vitamin C and provide about half the daily recommended allowance of vitamin A. Persimmons are relatively low in calories, about seventy-seven per fruit. The season for persimmons begins in October and runs through January.

Pineapples

The international symbol of welcome and hospitality is the pineapple. It originated in South America and was spread throughout the tropical areas of the world by the early explorers. In Hawaii, during the late 1700s, the pineapple was considered a weed and quite a nuisance. Around 1890, an Englishman, John Kidwell, cultivated the Hawaiian pineapple and set the foundation for the islands' largest industry (until tourism).

AVAILABLE *year-round*

The three sources that supply the U. S. market are Central America, Mexico, and Hawaii. Central America sends us the ***Red Spanish Pineapple.*** This pineapple has a lovely name but that's about all; I don't recommend it. Mexico ships the ***Sugar Loaf;*** this is the giant of pineapples, weighing from five to twelve pounds. When you find a ripe Sugar Loaf, its taste is as good as any other variety. One problem—Mexico has a tendency to ship unripened fruit, and pineapples do not ripen after being picked.

Hawaii grows and ships the best pineapple in the world, the ***Smooth Cayenne.*** This variety also grows in South Africa and the Philippines, but I doubt that you will find those two areas represented in your local garden grocery. However, during the mid-1980s, the Hawaiian Smooth Cayenne was transplanted with great success to Central America's Costa Rica, among other countries. When ripe, the Hawaiian Cayenne is the sweetest, juiciest pineapple in the world. The flavor and sweetness of this transplant to Central America has steadily improved to the point where most of the pineapples sold in the Southern United States and a large part of the East Coast are shipped from Central America. This is great for consumers because over the past ten years, the pineapple is among the few fruits that has experienced an overall drop in price.

There is one major difference between the Hawaiian and Central American Smooth Cayenne—shell (or skin) color. When ripe, the Hawaiian fruit has a beautiful golden tan shell. The Central American pineapple is green when ripe, but the farmers have been working to change the color. Personally, I hope they don't succeed; I think it is great to be able to tell the two pineapples apart.

Being a tropical fruit, pineapples are available year-round. When shopping, remember that shell color is not the most important thing. First, examine the crown (the green part that adorns the top of the fruit). It should be green with no dark or dry ends—those are the first signs of age. Next examine the body. Notice the little semi-circular sections of the fruit—they are called eyes. I like to say, "Pineapples are like kids—if you treat them badly, they will cry." Avoid any fruit with leaking eyes or bruises and mold.

The most important key to selecting the perfect pineapple, be it the golden ripe Hawaiian or the beautiful green Central American, is smell. A ripe pineapple gives off the most wonderful tropical aroma, so put your nose to work.

Like the kiwi and the papaya, the pineapple contains papain as well as chlorine, which aid in digestion. Those items also make the fruit a natural meat tenderizer; therefore, it is excellent in marinades and cooking with beef, pork, and chicken.

Pineapples provide a wealth of goodness: They are low in calories and high in vitamins A and C, low in fat and rich in calcium, phosphorus, and potassium.

CURTIS'S ALOHA PASTA SALAD

8 to 12 oz. of your favorite pasta, cooked

4 oz. snow peas

2 big broccoli tops

1/2 fresh pineapple, diced

1 Vidalia onion, diced

2 celery stalks, diced

1 can white tuna

4 to 6 oz. vinaigrette*

Steam snow peas and broccoli tops together about 4 minutes. Allow to cool. Mix all ingredients together. I think the salad is best when chilled.

*Use my recipe on page 164, minus the mustard, or your favorite.

Plums

This fruit has been around so long, its exact origin is unknown. There are types of plums native to North America, Europe, and Asia. The most noteworthy American variety, I would say, is the ***Sloe,*** used in the making of sloe gin. Let me tell you, I'm not much of a drinker, but in my early twenties I woke up on a few mornings feeling the effects of this fermented variety.

Luther Burbank, one of history's most famous horticulturists, is the father of the modern plum. (A note of interest, at least to me, is that the Southern California city of Burbank is named for him, and the northern California city of Santa Rosa is named for one of his most famous creations, the Santa Rosa plum.)

Botanically speaking, the fruit is a drupe (any fruit with a soft, fleshy part that has a seed and is covered with skin). Plums belong to the same family as nectarines and peaches, with sizes and shapes as numerous as the varieties (literally hundreds). They come in sizes as small as the tip of a finger to as large as a fist, and there are too many shapes to describe. As for colors, there are red, blue, yellow-green, purple, black, and orange (what a rainbow!).

By far the most popular plum commercially and in the backyard is the one Mr. Burbank created, the ***Santa Rosa.*** There are two varieties of these, the early and the late. The early Santa Rosa, which shows up on the market in the merry month of May (wait until the latter part of the month to make your first purchase), is round to oval in shape with a bit of a point. The color is a rusty red, which darkens to near black if left on the tree long enough. It's a good eating plum.

There is very little difference in the appearance of the late Santa Rosa and the early. The late matures and is ready for market from July through August. The big difference, I feel, is in the taste; because the later Rosa gets to ripen in all the summer sun, it has a sweeter taste. However, other produce people may disagree with me.

There are other varieties that do sell well and offer good flavor. First, there's a rich purple-skinned variety that is medium in size with an olive shape and pale yellow flesh; it's the **Tragedy.** The next variety has pretty much the same shape as the Tragedy, but it's much larger and the flesh color is a deeper yellow; this is the **Simka.** These two plums usually start to show up on the market in mid- to late-June.

The most popular mid-season variety is the **El Dorado.** Too bad it's not around during February, because it would make a great Valentine gift. It's a beautiful, heart-shaped plum with black skin, and the flesh is almost the color of fresh-cut redwood, with a nice sweet flavor.

Some of the latest plums to show up on the market are the new hybrid types, including the **Casselman,** the **Laroda,** and the quite popular **Queen Ann.** They are all rather large, round, reddish fruits.

Plums are available year-round. However, the domestic season begins in May and runs through September and October, with the season peaking in late June or early July through August, when flavor is best and prices are at their lowest.

When shopping for plums, regardless of variety, choose fruit with good color. By this I mean full color—be it red or yellow or black—from bottom to top. If the skin still shows green, that is a sign of immaturity, and the plum could lack flavor. The fruit should be firm but not rock hard, with a give to the touch. Soft fruit is okay, but it should not be spongy-soft. If you select soft fruit, use it that day—it's great in making sorbet.

Firm, ripe plums are good eating the day of purchase and will become soft-ripe in two or three days at room temperature. To slow the ripening process, place the fruit in the refrigerator. However, I don't like doing that until the plum is completely ripe.

Plums are an excellent source of vitamin A and a good source of vitamin C and protein. They are low in calories and fat, making them a great snack.

Pomegranates

When I was a child, I loved it when my parents would bring home pomegranates; it was like getting candy and a toy at the same time. I had so much fun trying to tear away the rather pretty, leathery skin without breaking open the honeycomb-like clusters that held the candy-sweet nectar of the pomegranate. As I got older, it didn't seem to be as much fun opening the fruit. I'm sure that is the reason this fruit has not enjoyed the popularity in America that it does in other parts of the world.

AVAILABLE
*September-
January*

Pomegranates are believed to have originated in the Mediterranean region and are still a very popular fruit in that area. Like apricots, this fruit was planted throughout California by the Spanish padres as they opened new missions on the West Coast. The tree is just beautiful. In summertime, its dark green leaves are a wonderful background for the bright orange flowers it produces. And in autumn, when the fruit ripens, it's as if God decided to decorate a Christmas tree a few months early.

When selecting pomegranates, choose large fruit that is heavy for its size, is free from cuts, and has no dark spots. The season begins in September and winds down in December or January. The fruit is rather moderate nutritionally. It contains a trace amount of vitamin A, some vitamin C (about four milligrams), and fair amounts of calcium and phosphorus.

To open a pomegranate, cut off the crown with a sharp knife. Make several shallow slices lengthwise down the fruit, being careful not to cut too deeply into the pomegranate. Next, place the scored fruit into a bowl of water and soak for five minutes. While holding the fruit in the water, break into sections, separating the seeds from the membrane with your fingers. The seeds will sink to the bottom; the membrane will float to the top. Discard the membrane, rinse and pat dry the seeds, then eat.

Quince

The quince originated in Asia and is not a new fruit. Although the quince now seems to be a forgotten fruit, during the early part of this century it was one of America's most popular produce items.

The quince, like the apple and pear, is a member of the rose family. Its fragrance is like a lovely perfume, and in the days before all the fancy air fresheners, many people kept a display of fresh quince in their homes just for the lovely aroma. As with apple and pear trees, the quince tree flowers in spring and its fruit ripens in fall; however, unlike its relatives, the quince is not very appetizing when eaten right off the tree or out of hand. When tree-ripened, the quince has a pretty, yellow skin, but the flesh is a pale color and extremely tart. No matter how much you enjoy tart fruit, like Granny Smith apples, I doubt you will enjoy the taste of raw quince.

However, when cooked, especially in a little syrup, the flesh becomes a pinkish color and much of the tartness disappears. Because of all the work people deem necessary to enjoy it, the quince has all but disappeared from retail stores in America. This is a shame, for preparing quince is not that hard; it's like making an apple pie without a crust. All you do is peel the fruit, core and slice it, season it with nutmeg and cinnamon if you like, add water and a little sugar, then simmer about forty-five minutes.

Fresh quince is usually available only during fall. Unfortunately, unless you have a tree in the backyard (which is common in the South), the only stores that carry them on a regular basis are the gourmet and specialty shops, so prices tend to be high.

When shopping for quince, choose firm, unbruised fruit with high yellow color. At home, the fruit will keep at least two weeks right on the counter.

The quince, while not as nutritious as the apple, does contain vitamin A and small amounts of vitamins B and C. It also provides calcium, iron, and phosphorus. When raw, quince is low in calories, but it requires sweetener when cooked.

Strawberries

The best strawberries I ever ate were grown in Norway. I was in a little town—Lillehammer—about 60 miles north of Oslo, where the 1994 Winter Olympics will be held. Few people would think of Norway as berry country with its relatively short growing season, but these berries were delicious! Across the street from where I stayed was a farm with a sign that read "All You Can Pick and Carry for 20 kroner" (then about four U. S. dollars). My friend and I picked about four gallons, and many of the berries were as big as tennis balls. The color was a beautiful red, dark but not auburn, and not as light as those wonderful Norwegian sunsets, which are just breathtaking. During that visit to the "Land of the Midnight Sun," I fell in love with eating strawberries and cream and have enjoyed that combination ever since.

AVAILABLE
year-round

Strawberries grow wild the world over, and their cultivation dates back hundreds of years. In Europe they were beautiful, but small and not too sweet. The berries native to North America had excellent flavor, but were still small. During the early 1700s European explorers found a rather large variety growing in South America. By cross-breeding the three types, botanists came up with the source of all the hybrid varieties we enjoy today, which include the **Hovey,** the first hybrid strawberry developed in the United States, and the **Wilson,** the **Heidi,** the **Chandler,** and the **Driscoll.**

California is by far the world's largest and best supplier of fresh strawberries. Strawberry production spans eleven months of the year, excluding only the month of December. Then, Florida steps in, and other berries arrive by air shipment from New Zealand. Both Florida and New Zealand produce fine berries.

Like pineapples, strawberries do not ripen further after being harvested; therefore, selection is very important. When shopping, choose dry, firm berries with rich color that covers the fruit up to the cap (which should always be green, a good sign of freshness). Avoid any berry with a dull or pale color (they are flavorless), and berries that are soft, wet, or showing mold. If stored in brown paper bags in the produce drawer of your refrigerator, strawberries can keep a week. However, to enjoy the best flavor and receive the most nutrition, you should consume them within three days.

The strawberry is an excellent skin-cleansing food, and it helps rid the body of harmful toxins. Fresh strawberries are high in vitamins A, B, and C, as well as containing large amounts (for their size, of course) of potassium and calcium.

Tangerines, Tangelos

AVAILABLE
October-
December

My favorite citrus fruits are in the mandarin family, which includes the tangerine, tangelo, and mandarin orange. In your local produce store you will very rarely see a display of mandarin oranges. With this in mind, let's concentrate on tangerines and tangelos.

In the produce business, we often use these names interchangeably, although they are different. Tangerine describes the smallest member of the mandarin family, while tangelo is used for the larger tangerines. The tangelo is the by-product of various citrus fruits and the tangerine. Tangelos are much larger than tangerines, but the skin is tight, which makes them much harder to peel. In Florida, four varieties of tangelos are grown. The **Mineola** is the one I recommend. (It is also known as the Red Tangelo and the Honeybell.) Mineolas are seedless, quite juicy, and very flavorful. This fruit is deep orange and much larger than the tangerine, and it has a rather pointed, stemmed end, which makes it easy to identify. I think the Mineola is one of the best citrus fruits of all.

The other three Florida tangelos are the **Early K,** the **Nova,** and the **Orlando.** The Early K is the first tangelo available each year; its season begins in October and ends mid-November. The

Early K looks very much like a tangerine; it's very juicy and has seeds, but the flavor makes me think of medicine. The season for the Novas and Orlandos begins in November; these varieties look just like the Early K, have about the same amount of seeds and juice, but are much sweeter.

Tangerines are the baby of the mandarin family. The size may be "baby," but the flavor is delicious. Of all the citrus groups, the tangerine has the best overall flavor. Most of the tangerines sold in the United States come from Florida. The two most popular varieties are **Dancy** and **Robinson.** Dancy is the smaller of the two, but it also has the sweetest flavor.

The Dancy and the Robinson are very good, and I'm sure you will enjoy both, but there are two other tangerines to put on your must-taste list: **Murcott** and the **Clementine.** In 1972, the name Murcott was changed to **Honey Tangerine.** The name fits the fruit; it's sweet as honey, and the flesh is beautiful. The skin color never becomes a total orange, but don't let that stop you from choosing this wonderful tangerine. Next is the Clementine. I really like that name, and the fruit even more. The Clementine is seedless, with a delightful flavor and a fine, smooth texture.

When shopping for tangerines and tangelos, don't worry so much about color, especially with Florida fruit. Because of the warm nights, the fruits almost never reach a deep orange color. The peel should be nice and tight with no sagging at the stem end (a sign of age). Also avoid fruit with mold or dark spots. Tangerines and tangelos are quite perishable, so handle with care. They should be stored in the refrigerator (up to a week) until you are ready to eat them.

Like the entire citrus family, tangelos and tangerines are high in vitamin C and contain fair amounts of vitamin A and potassium.

VEGETABLES

Artichokes

The artichoke is native to the Mediterranean region of southern Italy. Following its cultivation, the artichoke became a favorite crop of Italian farmers and a popular mealtime food throughout Italy. In fact, Italy is still the top-producing and top-consuming country of fresh artichokes in the world. French settlers introduced the artichoke to America, in the Louisiana Territory. The French learned of the unusual vegetable (which resembles a pinecone but is actually the flower of a plant related to the thistle) through Catherine de Medici. When de Medici left Italy to become queen of France, she brought with her Italian chefs and many of the food staples of Italy, one of which was the artichoke. Thus began a new era in French cuisine.

Although Italy leads the world in production, the best artichokes are grown right here in the United States—on the West Coast, about seventy miles south of San Francisco in the town of Castroville, California. Thanks to the warm days and cool, foggy nights and mornings, the nut-like flavor of the Castroville artichokes is surpassed nowhere on earth.

Artichokes are available year-round; however, the peak season for flavor runs March through May.

In selecting artichokes, choose whatever size you prefer. I love the baby artichokes that you can eat whole, including the chokes. The choke is the normally inedible thorny part between the paddles (leaves) and the heart, but it's so small on the baby artichokes that it is not noticeable. I also love the big ones because the heart is so much larger, and the heart is the best part. Choose artichokes that are heavy for their size, with tight heads. Don't worry if brown spots are present; most of the time they are caused by frost and have no bearing on the flavor.

As for the nutritional value of this unusual vegetable, the bad news is that they are rather high in sodium. The good news is that

AVAILABLE
year-round

DOMESTIC PEAK
March-May

artichokes are loaded with potassium and phosphorus as well as two vitamins which may surprise you, A and C.

Artichokes can be served hot or cold, with or without sauce or butter. If you want to cook them, it's easy. Just steam artichokes as you would broccoli or cauliflower, but longer—about forty minutes.

Most people think eating the vegetable is the hard part. Nonsense! All you do is pull off a leaf, dip it in sauce, and drag it between your teeth, discarding the portion that does not come off. The tiny inner leaves may be eaten entirely, and they are quite good. After all leaves have been removed, you will see a fuzzy center called the choke. This portion is not edible (except in baby artichokes); scoop it out with a spoon and discard it. Be careful not to dig too deep, though, because beneath the choke is the real prize, the heart, the most flavorful part of the artichoke.

Arugula

AVAILABLE
year-round

Rocket Salad, another name for arugula, is an important vegetable crop where it is indigenous: southern Europe and western Asia. The original name of the vegetable is *eruca sativa;* so where does the name of arugula come from, you wonder? After becoming one of the most popular salad greens throughout the Old World, *eruca sativa* made its way to Brazil, where it became just as popular and was called "rucula." In America, there have been minor changes in spelling and pronunciation, resulting in "arugula." Unfortunately arugula, although very popular in Italian-American neighborhoods, has yet to gain the widespread popularity it deserves. Arugula has a distinct flavor, pungent and tangy, that I really enjoy. Try fresh arugula in your next tossed green salad. This vegetable mixes well, raw or cooked, with tomato.

As I said, arugula has yet to gain widespread popularity on its own, but there is a new salad mixture called mescloon on the gourmet scene. It not only utilizes the beautiful green arugula leaves (which resemble oversized oak leaves or the green leaf attached to radishes); it also contains the attractive yellow flower of the mature arugula plant.

I first became aware of mescloon while living and working in New York, but my appreciation for this somewhat decadent mixture came on a recent visit to northern California. The mescloon mixture, sometimes marketed as "Baby Lettuce Mix," consists of the finest young and tender baby lettuces, such as **Red** and **Green Oak, Boston, Red** and **Green Leaf, Lollo Rosso, Biando Rosso, Mizuna** (a Japanese baby lettuce), and other expensive salad greens, such as arugula and its flower. During that California visit, I had the opportunity to dine at the exquisite Kenwood Restaurant, located in the Sonoma Valley. On the recommendation of the manager and my dear friend Jerry Cabral, I tried their house salad, featuring mescloon and sautéed goat cheese. The salad was divine!

When shopping for rocket salad or arugula (in some stores you may see it labeled as Italian watercress), choose whole leaves high in rich, green color, with no wilting around the edges. The vegetable is quite perishable, so try to purchase it on the day you plan to prepare it. Remember that because of the strong, pungent (but not overpowering) flavor, a little goes a long way. If you have to store arugula, wash it first in cold water, then wrap it in damp paper towels. Place that in a plastic bag and refrigerate for no more than two days.

Like the other green leaf vegetables, arugula is very high in vitamin A, phosphorus, and calcium. However, because of the small amount you will be consuming, I think the flavor is the biggest selling point.

Asparagus

AVAILABLE
year-round

**DOMESTIC
PEAK**
*February-
July*

In the produce business, we refer to this vegetable as "grass." The word "asparagus" in the ancient Greek tongue meant "shoot." A member of the beautiful lily family, asparagus is believed to have originated in Asia Minor or the eastern Mediterranean, two areas where this vegetable can still be found growing in its most primitive form.

Throughout the Roman Empire, asparagus was valued for its heavenly flavor and its medicinal powers. The Romans believed asparagus could cure toothaches and heart ailments, among other things. They developed many recipes and potions that used fresh and dried asparagus. Roman farmers also worked hard to improve their cultivation techniques and kept extensive records of their progress.

For produce people, asparagus used to be the first sign of spring, making a light debut late in February. By the end of April, or by mid-May, the crop was at full tilt, winding down at the end of July. Today, with improved refrigeration, jet shipments from the southern hemisphere, and stronger varieties, asparagus is available year-round.

During January, the bulk of the asparagus sold in the United States comes from Chile, Mexico, and New Zealand. In February, the first domestic crop comes on line from California, where the season stretches through summer. During mid-summer, Washington and Michigan crops are available. Toward the end of fall, a second Mexican crop is available, taking up the slack of fading domestic production. Through the remainder of fall and part of winter, Chile and New Zealand asparagus are again sold.

There are two types of asparagus available—green and white (actually off-white). The only real difference is in the color. The white aspargus is kept in darkness to prevent photosynthesis, whereas the green asparagus is grown in full sunlight. The tastes are virtually identical.

When shopping for fresh asparagus, always choose stalks that are straight and rich in color. The tops should be closed tightly. Some people prefer large asparagus, but personally, I've found the smaller the stalk, the better the flavor, and the vegetable is less stringy. When asparagus is past its peak, it will let you know. The tops will be open, and if there is a slightly foul odor, avoid the vegetable.

Store the asparagus no more than five days in the refrigerator in a tightly closed paper bag. Try to use it within three days of purchase.

Asparagus is extremely nutritious. It's high in vitamins A, B, and C. It is also rich in calcium, protein, and potassium.

Beans

I guess we could say beans are truly the international vegetable, for they are grown in virtually every country on earth. There are dozens of varieties of beans, and each seems to have a different homeland.

Africa has been home to the **fava bean** for centuries. In America, this large, flat bean is often called "horse bean" or "broad bean." They sometimes grow to lengths of twenty inches. I had always thought they were native to Italy because there are many great Italian fava dishes, such as this one:

AVAILABLE
varieties,
year-round

FAVA BEANS

2 lbs. shelled fava
  beans
3 Tbl. margarine or
  olive oil
1 clove garlic, chopped
  fine
1 small onion, chopped
1 lb. Jerusalem arti-
  chokes, peeled and
  diced

Boil fava beans until tender, about one to two hours. Drain; let cool. In a frying pan, add margarine or oil, garlic, and onions. Cook until onions are transparent. Add artichokes and cook until golden brown, about ten to fifteen minutes. Now add fava beans. Cook until they are thoroughly heated. Add salt and pepper to taste, then serve.

The North and South American continents are home to **Lima** and **Snap Beans** (or green beans), two of my favorites. When I was a child, Mama called green beans "string beans." As I grew older I found out that everyone else called them string beans as well because of the string-like fiber that runs down the seam of the bean, which must be removed before cooking. But with today's hybrid varieties, strings are no longer a bother. The ten-to-twelve-inch, flat, improved **Kentucky Wonder** variety is very popular in fresh and frozen markets. Some other favorites are the round **Blue Lake** and **Harvester.** They grow to be about half the size of the Kentucky Wonder, but I think their flavor is a little smoother, and their texture is less tough.

There are other snap beans to look for in the '90s. First, there's the **Yellow Wax Bean.** Except for color, it could be a twin to the Blue Lake. These beans were once quite popular, then were pushed aside, and now they are making a comeback as a gourmet item.

The second to look for is the **Purple Snap.** With the ever-increasing American fancy for colorful foods, the purple snap is destined to be a hit. The flavor and texture are very similar to those of the Yellow Wax and Blue Lake beans, and they are also a great conversation piece at dinnertime or parties.

The **Lima Bean** is an old American favorite. On a national scale, fresh lima beans are almost a thing of the past (why, is a mystery to me), but in the South they are still quite popular during summer. If you are able to find them, give them a try. You will truly enjoy the unique flavor and texture of these beans.

Chinese Long Beans (see Oriental Vegetables) of course originated in Asia. Here in America, they are sometimes called "yard-long beans."

Romano, or Italian beans are called "bush beans" in the South. These beans have a wild look and are irregular in shape: some are flat, some are wide, and some are even curled—but all are tasty. They are wonderful cooked with chicken stock and diced onions. The Italian bean grows to about seven inches long. They are very popular internationally, but in America they are popular only in the South.

Cranberry Beans are one of the most beautiful to look at, and very tasty. In Mexico and the West Indies, they are a huge favorite. The pod looks like something Andy Warhol would have designed: it's off-white and speckled, with pinkish red tints—just beautiful. Then when you open up the pod, the beans match the pods in color, though sometimes they are a little more red than white.

Fresh cranberry beans start to appear in August. Try this recipe:

CRANBERRY BEANS

Place all ingredients in a heavy sauce pan; add 2 quarts of water. Cook over medium heat until beans are tender, about 2 hours, and of course, season to taste.

2 lbs. shelled cranberry beans

1 medium onion, chopped

2 cloves garlic, chopped

2 medium tomatoes, chopped

2 Tbl. olive oil

salt and pepper to taste

These beans are more familiar in their dried form, called "red beans," which are very popular in Louisiana.

Another variety is the **haricots verts,** or **French beans,** which look like miniature snap beans. When I was growing up, I had canned beans of this type, which can't touch fresh French beans when prepared properly. Now you may have to go to a gourmet shop or farmers' market to find fresh *haricots verts,* but it is well worth the effort.

Beans are a good source of vitamin A, riboflavin, and a wealth of minerals, as well as being low in fat.

When shopping for fresh beans of any variety, let your eye and touch be the guide. Look for fresh beans—those that have good color and no dark spots on either end. The bean should feel soft, almost moist. You never want to select stiff or hard beans, for those are two sure signs of age.

Fresh beans are fairly perishable, and they should be used as soon as possible. However, if stored properly in a tightly closed paper bag, they will keep for up to a week in your refrigerator. Most beans are available year-round. Bush beans may not be available in the winter, but most of the other types are.

Beets

Now here is a vegetable that the American consumer has all but forgotten. Before the days of high-speed refrigerated trucks and air cargo planes, which get our fresh produce from source to retail outlet in days, and some cases hours, retailers were more dependent on local or regional suppliers. Of course product availability was seasonal. In those days, beets were popular with retailers because they could be sold with their green tops during spring, summer, and fall, and the sweet beet root was available during the coldest months of winter. Now, however, although beets are still a major crop in this country (grown in more than thirty states), the majority of those are sold to processors to be bottled, canned, or used on salad bars.

In kitchens of days gone by, fresh beets were prized for several reasons. First, taste. The pleasant sweetness goes very well with meats and other vegetables. Today, with the new hybrid beets, the flavor is even better, so if shoppers would just try fresh beets, I'm sure this vegetable's popularity would soar again. Also available are baby beets, which are absolutely delicious and make great conversation pieces at dinner parties when served raw on a vegetable tray. **Candy Cane** and **Golden** are two baby varieties.

Another reason that beets were so popular is that their green tops are an excellent substitute for spinach, cooked or in salads. Many European restaurants distinguish between the beet roots and the beet tops, something I would like to see American restaurants do. There are many wonderful recipes for beet tops as well as beet roots.

When shopping for fresh beets, always select firm, medium-to-small vegetables because the larger the beet, the more likely it is to be dried out or woody in texture. The tops should be a bold green and, of course, not wilted. After purchasing, remove the green top

AVAILABLE
year-round

from the beet roots because those tops could extract moisture and dry out the root.

Nutritionally, beets are loaded; they are high in calcium, phosphorus, and protein. Indeed, we could call beets the blood food, for they furnish many nutrients needed to build red blood corpuscles.

Broccoli

AVAILABLE
year-round

The second most popular member of the cabbage family, and one of the most popular vegetables over all, is broccoli. This vegetable is another of the old-timers. The ancient Greeks and Romans are credited with its cultivation some two thousand years ago. From Italy, broccoli was introduced to France, then England, then on to the New World. Although this vegetable was brought to America early in our history, it took some 150 years to transform broccoli from an ethnic Italian vegetable to the mainstream produce we think of today. In 1920, a group of farmers, led by the D'Arrigo brothers in northern California, decided to ship a sample load of broccoli back east, as well as to advertise this wonderful, nourishing produce via the new craze of that era—radio. Since then, broccoli's popularity has steadily grown.

California is by far the largest producer of what I called, as a child, "baby trees." That state's output accounts for over 85 percent of the annual broccoli crop marketed in America, and I have to give California an overall edge as far as quality is concerned, too. It seems that the area between San Francisco in the north and Santa Barbara in the south, with its warm days and fairly cool nights, is perfect for broccoli cultivation.

Other states that produce commercial broccoli include Arizona, Oregon, and Texas. Over the past few years I have seen steady improvement in the Texas crop, and the price is always competitive. Don't be afraid to ask produce people where their broccoli comes from.

There are two key factors to consider when shopping for fresh broccoli: touch and appearance. Always choose firm, heavy broccoli that has a nice green color with buds or florettes that are tightly compact. Some varieties have a purple tint, which is a sign of quality. Avoid broccoli that is limp or whose florettes have started to open, showing yellow flowers in the top. These are signs that the broccoli has passed its flavorful peak and has lost much of its nutritional value. Broccoli is fairly perishable, so it should be used within three days after purchasing. Broccoli, like other members of the cabbage family, is an excellent source of vitamins A and C.

Brussels Sprouts

Brussels sprouts are the newest member of the cabbage family. They were first discovered about three hundred years ago, and the name gives away their place of origin, Brussels, Belgium.

AVAILABLE
year-round

When I was a child, I thought this vegetable came from a strange cabbage that had little baby cabbages growing all around it. I must say I enjoyed looking at them much more than I did eating them. Now, after having seen them growing in the fields near Monterey, California, and on Long Island, New York, I think they remind me more of a collard stalk, except that there aren't as many greens at the top. All up and down the base of the plant are rows filled with what look like miniature cabbages. I guess my childhood imagination was pretty good, except that instead of the cabbages being on the ground, they are on the stalk.

According to the experts, here is how to buy them. The smaller the sprout the better the taste; anything over two or two-and-a-half inches in diameter is considered too large. Always choose firm vegetables with a nice green color, and avoid those with wilting yellowish leaves, black spots, or little holes in the sprout. These are all signs of age or indications that insects may have infected that particular vegetable. One last note about choosing Brussels sprouts: put your nose to work. Overly mature vegetables give off a very strong odor, much like spoiled cabbage.

As for nutrition, Brussels sprouts are loaded—high in vitamins A, B, and C, high in protein, and low in calories. They have a low fat count and are an excellent source of calcium, iron, and potassium.

Cabbage

AVAILABLE
year-round

The cabbage is one of the most ancient vegetables still grown today. Its cultivation dates back four thousand years, yet it remains among the top in popularity and sales to this date. Some one million tons are sold annually in the United States, and the only vegetables we buy in greater quantities are potatoes, lettuce, and tomatoes.

Head cabbage comes in two colors: green and red (sometimes called purple). There is no variety of white cabbage. I once got a phone call from someone raised in upstate New York. She was upset because she could not find what she called New York white cabbage down South. I explained to her that there was no variety of white cabbage; she was looking for stored cabbage.

Remember: to receive the most nourishment from fresh vegetables, they should be consumed raw.

Green cabbage is sometimes called "new cabbage" in produce circles because of the new green leaves that cover its head. As green cabbage ages, its color fades. Now in the farm areas of New York State and other northern regions where the winters are cold, it is a common practice to store cabbage in cold, dark barns. When this (old) cabbage reaches the market in the dead of winter, it is hard as a rock and almost bleached white. This old cabbage is great in cole slaw and for boiling, or anything else you would use the new green cabbage for, though its nutritional value may not be as high because of the aging factor.

Fresh cabbage may be as nourishing as any other single fruit or vegetable. It is an excellent source of calcium, phosphorus, and potassium, plus vitamins A, B, and C. (Remember: to receive the most nourishment from fresh vegetables, they should be consumed raw.)

The cooler months—when lettuce prices soar—are an excellent time to try a fresh cabbage salad. Here is a mix I highly recommend:

FRESH CABBAGE SALAD

Combine shredded cabbage, red or green, with finely chopped apples, using fresh-squeezed orange juice as your dressing. Of course, you could add some nuts to that salad for crunch and added protein.

1/2 head cabbage
2 medium apples
1 cup orange juice

When selecting fresh cabbage, always choose firm heads that are heavy for their size. Stay away from cabbage that the produce person has trimmed. Cabbage is high in vitamin C, but each time it is cut or trimmed, some vitamin C is lost.

Napa Cabbage

Napa cabbage is sometimes called "Chinese cabbage" because until a few years ago, fresh napa could only be found in Oriental markets. Its other common name is "celery cabbage," although this vegetable does not resemble celery at all, in taste or appearance.

I use this vegetable quite often; it's fantastic raw or cooked. Raw napa is a great addition to any tossed salad. In fact, I suggest making your next tossed salad with napa instead of lettuce. You'll find a pleasant sweet taste in this dish. As a cooked vegetable, napa blends well with other foods, especially chicken and potatoes, and it makes a nice cole slaw.

Nutrition and health experts believe cabbage helps prevent certain cancers. Napa is high in vitamins C and D. Although it has a sweet taste, it is lower in calories than the more familiar head cabbage.

When selecting napa cabbage, choose cabbage that feels heavy and has leaves with a nice, fresh appearance, with no bruises. Napa cabbage looks like romaine lettuce, but it has a lighter green color.

Carrots

AVAILABLE
year-round

This ancient vegetable was being cultivated hundreds of years before the birth of Christ, but its exact origin is unknown. Various sources say Afghanistan, Japan, or the Mediterranean. Whatever their origin, carrots have been popular throughout the world for centuries.

You may know the carrot as a common, ordinary vegetable. Well, let this garden grocer tell you, carrots are not so ordinary. They have a colorful past, which continues in some parts of the world. The early Dutch farmers grew large purple carrots, and the present-day farmers of northern Africa and Egypt still cultivate a small version of that variety, which I'm sure will be available in American markets soon. Fifteenth-century European farmers grew yellow carrots.

During the sixteenth century, the orange carrot made its debut in England and almost instantly became a food staple. Further, trendsetting Englishwomen thought the green carrot tops were so attractive that they used them to decorate their hats and often braided them into their hair.

The first Europeans to settle in America were pleasantly surprised to find that carrots were a well-established crop in their new homeland. In fact, if they had not had carrots to eat during the brutal winter of 1609, the people of Jamestown, Virginia, would have starved.

Today, carrots remain a popular vegetable; however, I think sales would soar if growers and processors would do just a little more marketing. We know carrots are great in salads and as vegetable sticks, but few realize how wonderful cooked carrots are. Try these easy ideas: sliced carrots sautéed in butter and brown sugar, or steamed with salt, pepper, and fresh dill. For meat eaters, the next time you broil beef or pork, do it on a bed of carrots (you can also cook chicken and fish that way), but remember to drain off the fat before eating.

Carrots are available in retail stores every day of the year. The best quality comes from California, the next best from Arizona, then Texas. Those three states are in production twelve months a year. Florida is another large producer of carrots, but I'm not a big fan of that sunshine crop; often the carrots are bitter, with a wood-like texture. During spring and summer, other eastern states and Canada produce market-quality carrots, but they aren't nearly as sweet as the western carrots.

Remember your mother saying, "Eat all your carrots so you can see well"? A single carrot, six to eight inches long, will supply more than six thousand units of vitamin A, well above the daily recommended requirement. This vitamin is essential in developing strong bones and teeth as well as maintaining healthy eyes. Carrots also contain vitamins B, C, D, E, and K, and remain low in calories, about forty calories per carrot.

When shopping for carrots choose firm, clean vegetables no more than eight inches long and two inches in diameter. If tops are attached, remove them as soon as possible because they will draw moisture from the carrot, causing bitterness and drying. Then place the carrots in a plastic bag and store in your refrigerator. Unfortunately, most carrots are sold in prepackaged one- and two-pound colored plastic bags. Do yourself a favor and peek through the bag, making sure there is no sprouting at the top of the carrot, and no wilting at the bottom end. Both are signs of age.

Over the past ten years, I've seen an increase in the popularity of the miniature carrots (about three inches long). In some areas—New York and Los Angeles, for instance—they're called French or Belgian carrots. There is nothing new about them; it's just that we Americans have finally caught up with the Europeans in appreciating smaller vegetables. Any of the recipes for standard carrots will work with the miniature ones, and I do think miniature carrots are much better cooked than raw.

Cauliflower

AVAILABLE
year-round

The word "cauliflower" means "cabbage flower," and this vegetable is the most elegant and delicate member of the cabbage family. For those reasons, it is also the most expensive. I say the cauliflower is elegant because its appearance is so pleasing. The beautiful snow-white or ivory inner portions of the vegetable are referred to as the curd. During the '90s, that term may have to be dropped because other varieties of cauliflower are being developed that produce green and purple heads. The flavors are just as pleasing as that of the familiar snowball varieties.

The white varieties account for more than 90 percent of all the cauliflower sold in the United States. There are a couple of reasons why I feel the colorful varieties will make drastic cuts into those percentages and will help cauliflower rival broccoli for the position of second most popular member of the cabbage family. First, cooking time is less for the green and purple cauliflower than the white—about the same as for broccoli. Second, we Americans are truly colorful people. During the '80s, although cauliflower has been around as long as broccoli (some twenty centuries), it was as if we had just discovered the vegetable. Now that we have discovered it and like it, the next step is to add colorful cauliflower to our evening meals, our crudités (raw vegetables), and our salads.

If you are wondering why I describe cauliflower as delicate, how many vegetables do you know of that need to wear a jacket? When cauliflower is being raised in the field, its white curd is blanketed by green leaves. That is called the jacket, which protects the delicate inner portion from the hot, dry sunlight of day and the cool, sometimes freezing temperatures at night. Because of the vegetable's delicacy, it takes a very good farmer to raise a marketable cauliflower, and that is why it is the most expensive member of the cabbage family.

The green leaves of the cauliflower jacket are edible. Their flavor reminds me of collard greens. When I worked out of the South San Francisco Produce Market, which is relatively close to the Salinas Valley, a major production area of cauliflower, I was able to purchase what was called "naked cauliflower." Naked cauliflower is untrimmed, with its jacket fully attached and free of the familiar plastic wrap we see in the supermarket. I wish for the consumer's sake that packing houses would ship some of the naked cauliflower to the markets east of California so that easterners could enjoy those wonderful greens attached to the cauliflower.

Like the other members of the cabbage family, cauliflower is extremely nutritious, high in both vitamins A and C, yet low in calories (as long as you do not add butter). This vegetable is also a good source for iron, phosphorus, and calcium.

When shopping for cauliflower, you probably will not find the naked pack, but if you do, look for a colorful jacket—green with a clean white center that leads to the base of the vegetable. Pull back the jacket to inspect the curd, making sure it is tightly packed. A spreading curd is a sign of age. For the more familiar plastic-wrapped cauliflower, choose a firm vegetable that has high color—clean white or ivory in the snowball varieties, nice green or purple in the colored varieties. If brown or dark spots are present, that vegetable should be discarded, as these are signs of age. One other tip: to be sure you have selected a fresh cauliflower, turn the package over and press the bottom stem. If it is soft, that is another sign of age.

Cauliflower will keep up to a week in the refrigerator, but for best flavor and nutrition, try to to consume it within three days of purchasing.

Celeriac

AVAILABLE
year-round

DOMESTIC PEAK
fall-winter

Most commonly called "celery root" or "celery knob," celeriac is a type of celery grown for its root. The green tops are too stringy and tough to eat raw, although when available, they work well in soups. In northern Europe the variety remains very popular, as it was in the U.S. before World War II.

If I had to guess the cause of the vegetable's decline in popularity, I'd say looks—it's one of the ugliest things in the produce department. Most are shipped to market when about the size of a baseball, but in different shapes. The color is a bit lighter than Mississippi mud, and it has bumps all over, like it's breaking out with acne, with a very thick and tough skin. Speaking of the skin, celery root is one of the few produce items that needs to be peeled before consuming.

Once the skin is removed, the inner beauty and outstanding flavor shine through. The flesh is soft and white with a smooth, string-free texture, making celery root great as a raw vegetable— useful in salads, for dipping, or just out of hand. It's also a delightful cooked vegetable, be it sautéed with onions or other items, added to soups, or battered and fried a la tempura. As with many root vegetables, I think with a little marketing and a few new recipes, celery root could regain much of the popularity it has lost over the past fifty years.

Celery root is available year-round. If there is a peak season, I'd say it's during the fall and winter months. If this vegetable has a down time, it's the summer months.

When shopping for celeriac, look for baseball-sized vegetables. A little bigger is okay, but not too much bigger. When celery root is too large, it sometimes has a hollow middle, and the texture becomes woody and tough. The outside should be clean and firm; if it's soft, that's a sign of age, and there could be decay. Sprouting is another sign of age, so both sprouting and soft roots should be avoided.

Celery root will keep literally weeks under refrigeration, although I don't recommend keeping the vegetable that long. After the root has been cut, try to use it within three days.

Like the common bunch celery, celeriac is low in calories and a good source for protein, calcium, potassium, and phosphorus.

The next time you use a recipe that calls for diced or chopped celery, try celeriac. The flavor is a bit stronger but not overpowering, and I think you will like it.

Celery

This member of the parsley family originated in the Mediterranean region long before the birth of Christ. The early Romans and Greeks did not consume celery as food; they used the vegetable as medicine. As a kid I hated celery in mama's potato salad, in stuffing, or in soups. But now, as an adult, I love it—even raw.

AVAILABLE *year-round*

Although there are many varieties of celery, they can be broken down into two types, white and green. The first was marketed under the names "blanched," "golden," or "golden heart" celery. I say "was" because the white celery has pretty much disappeared from the majority of retail outlets. The green type accounts for 99 percent of the celery sold annually. Again, there are many varieties of green celery. However, in the wholesale world of produce all green celery is called **Pascal**. At the store, don't concern yourself with names; there you'll just see the word "celery."

Celery is available year-round, with California and Florida being the major shippers. If there is a down time for the domestic crop, it's the late fall and winter; prices do climb during those months. But when broken down into cost per serving, celery, even during winter, is a good buy.

When shopping for celery, let your eyes be your guide. Look for freshness and rich, green color, with no darkness at the top, where the bunch was trimmed, or at the bottom, where it was cut from the root. Darkness is a sign of age. Also look for well-shaped bunches that are firm but not rock-hard and that show a lot of green in the middle. Limpness is another sign of age, and if the celery shows too much white in the middle, the bunch will lack flavor.

To store celery, place the vegetable in a paper bag, then refrigerate it. It will keep up to a week, but try to use it within three or four days to get the best flavor and nutritional value. If your celery becomes limp before you use it, cut off the bottom, put the stalks in water, and give them an hour or so to revitalize.

As for nutritional value, celery contains good amounts of vitamin C and protein, is low in calories (about twenty-five per bunch), and contains very little fat. It's a great source of calcium, phosphorus, and potassium.

My favorite soup stock is made by juicing one or two bunches of celery, then seasoning with salt, pepper, and herbs.

Chayote

I've got a feeling this vegetable is going to be very popular in the '90s. In Latin America, where chayote originated, some call it "pear vegetable" because of its shape and semisweet taste, but I think it looks more like an avocado. In other parts of South America, the vegetable is called "mango squash"; like the mango it has one flat seed that adheres tightly to the flesh that surrounds it. It is also called "mirliton," and the Cajuns and Creoles of Louisiana refer to it as "Melleteu." A Louisiana native said to me, "Melleteu grows like weeds down here so we cook it with everything."

AVAILABLE
year-round

DOMESTIC PEAK
October-March

Although the taste is semisweet, I doubt you would enjoy raw chayote by itself, though it is good used in salads or for dipping, and it mixes well with other foods, complementing their flavor. It is also delicious sautéed with beef, chicken, or fish, and it does not lose its crunchiness after being cooked.

When shopping for chayote (which is pronounced chä yo' tee), choose firm vegetables that are rich in color (nice green) and free of bruises.

Being a tropical vegetable, chayote is available virtually year-round, with its peak season being October through March. These vegetables are usually marketed with a recipe attached to give you more cooking ideas.

Chayote provides vitamin A and some potassium and is very low in calories. This squash stores well; it can be kept up to a week, unwrapped, in the refrigerator.

Chicory

AVAILABLE
year-round

When you say the word "chicory," most people think of a curly, leafy vegetable—endive or escarole. However, in reality "chicory" is the name of a family of vegetables that includes not only endive and escarole, but also radicchio.

The chicory family has been around a long time. It's believed to have originated in southern Europe. Ground chicory roots were used in a brewed drink long before coffee beans were heaped into a pot. In fact, you can still find ground chicory root in specialty stores, particularly down around New Orleans.

Endive or escarole is the crown of the chicory plant. It's called "curly chicory" in the east, and out west the same vegetable is called "endive" or "curly endive." I started my produce business in northern California and ran it for about six years before moving to New York; during my first few weeks in the Big Apple, that name difference caused me so much trouble! When a customer asked for chicory I thought he or she was referring to the whole family and gave that customer any member of the family I had available. My boss didn't understand until I explained the chicory family tree to him and the rest of the employees.

Endive is used in America primarily in salads. In Europe, it's also used as a cooked item. I've tried them cooked, and they're not bad.

On first sight, endive looks like green leaf lettuce, but on closer inspection one sees that it's just the outer leaves that are green; the middle portion of the vegetable is white or yellow. The texture is much tougher or grassy-like, the flavor a little on the bitter side, though this vegetable mixes well with other greens in salad.

Escarole is a wide-leaf chicory that looks very much like curly endive. It has green outer leaves that lighten toward the middle. The texture is not as tough as that of endive, nor is the taste as bitter. It looks great added to any salad, and it also makes a nice cooked vegetable.

Radicchio, sometimes called "red chicory" or "Italian red lettuce," is as common in Italy as iceberg lettuce is here. Radicchio comes in many shapes and shades of red; it is the head-forming member of the chicory family. It looks like a small head of light red cabbage with a white base and white streaks running through it (like the marble meat eaters look for in steak). Radicchio sells for as high as nine dollars a pound, mainly because the majority of what is sold in American retail stores is imported from Italy—although there are some growers in the States.

The chicory family is available year-round and except for radicchio, it sells at pretty reasonable prices.

When shopping for chicory, remember that freshness is the key. Choose bunches with nice green leaves, and remember that smaller bunches usually offer a better taste. Avoid bunches with wilted leaves and any that show insect spots or that have been heavily trimmed.

Members of the chicory family will keep in the refrigerator two to three days. It's best to place them in a paper bag. As I always say, try to use them as soon as possible.

The members of the chicory family are very high in vitamin A. They contain a fair amount of vitamin C and supply phosphorus, potassium, iron, and calcium. They're low in fat and calories.

Corn

AVAILABLE
year-round

**DOMESTIC
PEAK**
*late May-
September*

Corn is one of the true American food crops. Maize (the Native American name for this grain) originated in South America and was well established throughout the Americas long before the first European settlers ventured west. I read that Columbus and his crew members were astonished to see corn growing in fields that spread ten miles and more. Not only was the taste of this new grain a pleasant surprise, but also the sailors quickly took to another corn product: the cigars made by Native Americans, using corn husks as wrappers.

The Pilgrims were introduced to maize almost as soon as they climbed off the *Mayflower.* In fact, they named the crop "Indian corn." Later that was shortened simply to "corn," which in Europe means "grain." The very trusting and friendly natives taught the Pilgrims everything they knew about planting maize, fertilizing it with fish, harvesting it, grinding it into flour, and saving and storing seed to plant the following season. It makes you wonder. If those Native Americans had had a crystal ball, would they have been so willing to teach the settlers everything they knew about the amazing grain crop?

Today, hundreds of varieties of corn are grown in this country alone, and those crops are a long way from the wild grasses related to wheat and barley that sprang up in South America in pre-Columbian days. Although there are numerous varieties, from a commercial standpoint there are only two types. Field corn stays on the stalk and dries before harvesting. It is used in making flour, corn oil, and feed for livestock as well as seed for future crops. Sweet corn is the type we buy fresh, frozen, and in cans.

Frankly, I don't think the variety is very important. I know we all have our regional favorites—like **Silver Queen** or **Golden Bantam** or **Country Gentleman**—but unless you know the farmer, the shipper, and the wholesaler, I doubt you will know the exact variety that is in your retail outlet.

So what do you look for when shopping for fresh corn? First, ask your produce person what day the corn arrived; if it was more than three days ago, pass. Next, examine the husk for color. It should be evenly green, with no darkness at the bottom. That is a sign of age. The top should be free of worm holes or decay. Don't worry about the golden silk, because if it gets just a little moisture on it, it will blacken or fall off. Finally, pull back the husk to examine the kernels. Do not squeeze them with your finger, for that will damage that ear of corn. Just examine the kernels carefully to see if they are plump and full. When corn starts to dry out, it sags at the top and there are noticeable dents in the top portion of that kernel.

Fresh corn is available year-round, but the peak season begins in late May and runs through September. Wait until June or July to try one of my favorite ways to enjoy corn—raw. There is nothing as good as one of those sweet, yellow ears of corn, so plump and juicy.

Generally, fresh corn should be purchased on the day you are going to use it, unless you intend to freeze it. As soon as corn is picked, the sugar begins to convert into starch.

Corn is nutritionally well-rounded, providing fair amounts of both vitamins A and B plus riboflavin, calcium, and phosphorus. Some may think it's a bit high in calories, about one hundred per ear.

Corn-off-the-Cob is a piece of cake! Use a bundt or tube cake pan. Stick the shucked ear of corn in the center pan opening, push the knife down the sides of the ear and the kernels will fall in the pan.

Cucumber

AVAILABLE
year-round

I don't think you will be surprised when I say this vegetable belongs to the same botanical family as the summer squash (zucchini, yellow squash, etc.), for when you look at them, you can see the family resemblance. What might be surprising (to you city folks) is that this same family has as relatives the sweet melons: honeydew, cranshaw, and the others. If you find that hard to believe, then next spring or early summer try to get out to a farm area (or a nursery) and ask to see the cucumber plant. Then look at the melon vines. You'll see they're hard to tell apart. As with so many produce items, there are dozens of varieties of cucumber; however, for our purposes, we'll break them into three groups.

First there are the ugly little bumpy-skinned pickling cucumbers, which aren't very big sellers outside the southern part of the country. (We make a lot of homemade sweet and dill pickles down South.) I'm not really what you would call a cucumber fan, but I do enjoy these little ones fresh as well as pickled. What they lack in looks, they more than make up for in flavor.

Second is what's commonly called the smooth-skinned type. It's the kind most popular in retail stores. They are dark green in color and come to market when 6 to 8 inches long. Unfortunately, this type of cucumber is one of the most heavily waxed items in the produce section; maybe that's why I'm not so hot on "cukes."

Finally, we have the English, European, or Hot House type. This is that long vegetable that's wrapped in cellophane. I think I like that plastic better than the wax on other cukes. The English cuke is semi-seedless. Personally, I prefer these cooked rather than raw.

Cucumbers are available year-round, and they are produced in virtually every state in the union; Florida, California, and Texas are all major shippers. During the winter, when there is a drop—

though not a full halt—in domestic production, we import large amounts of cucumbers from Mexico.

When shopping for cukes, look for ones that are heavy for their size and have a firm, rich green color (except for the pickling cukes, which have a duller green color and are not as shapely as the other two types). The weight lets you know the vegetable is juicy. Avoid puffed-up vegetables, as that's a sign that the cuke has passed its peak. If the cucumber shows heavy wrinkles or is shriveled at the ends, those are stay-away signs. Remember, let your eyes guide you; most of the time with cucumbers, if they look good, they are good.

Cucumbers provide vitamins A and C. They are low in calories and fat and are good sources for potassium and calcium.

Eggplant

Eggplant is one of a few vegetables not at its nutritional best when eaten raw. In fact, eggplant should never be consumed raw since it is a member of the nightshade family, which includes some poisonous plants. Raw eggplant could cause illness.

AVAILABLE
year-round

This subtropical jewel originated centuries ago in India and China, where it remains extremely popular today. Arabian traders took the vegetable westward to Turkey, where it spread to Greece and then to Spain and, in the sixteenth century, to Italy. Eggplant seeds are believed to have been brought to America by Spanish explorers; whatever the case, eggplants were found in the southern part of this country, an ideal growing area. That explains why Florida was, and still is, the number-one producer of eggplant in the United States.

There are many varieties of eggplant. In the common globe

shape there are *New York, Black Magic,* and *Black Beauty* eggplants. They all are deep purple, almost black in color. The medium globe or *Italian* eggplant has that same color but is about half the size of the common varieties; other medium eggplants include the French *Bonde de Valence,* a round eggplant; Puerto Rican *Rayada,* a purple-and-white striped eggplant; and Italian *Rosa Bianco,* another purple-and-white one. Some of the white varieties, which come in all shapes and sizes, are the *Chinese, Casper, White Egg, Easter Egg,* and *Thia Round Turtle Egg.* Then there are the green varieties, which are also egg-shaped; my two favorites are the *Applegreen,* about the size of a small Granny Smith apple, and the *Green Thia,* which comes in bunches and looks like green grapes.

Although there are many types of eggplant, they have only three basic differences: size, shape, and color. Some will argue that the flavor is different in the smaller eggplant, but I feel the major difference between the small and large eggplant is that the small ones have fewer seeds, which makes the texture smoother when cooked.

Being a subtropical vegetable, eggplant is available year-round. When shopping, look for firm, bright, shiny eggplant that is free of scars or dark spots. When eggplant has been mistreated, it will show (those dark spots), so avoid bruised eggplant. Another sign of freshness is the stem end. First, it should always be on the eggplant, for if it has been removed, the retailer is trying to hide something—age, to be exact. Second, the stem should be a rich green color; if it is not, it too is old and should be avoided. That goes for all eggplants, including the white varieties.

For those of you trying to cut back on your red meat intake, eggplant is a great substitute. It offers a fair amount of protein, is low in calories, and is high in potassium, calcium, and phosphorus.

EASY EGGPLANT

Wash eggplant and remove cap (peel if desired). Cut into small pieces about 1" square. Salt and let drain in a colander about 20 minutes. Pat dry and place in a baking pan. Mix garlic with oil and pour over eggplant. Bake in preheated 400 degree degree oven until eggplant is tender and brown. Cool and place in a bowl. Mix in vinegar, wine, and pepper to taste. Makes an excellent salad and is great with rice or pasta as a side dish or main dish.

2 medium eggplants
5 Tbl. salt
2 tsp. minced garlic
1/2 cup oil
1/3 cup vinegar
1/3 cup white wine
pepper

Garlic

This member of the onion family is believed to have originated in Asia thousands of years ago. In addition to its ability to add excellent flavors to various cuisines, mystic and curative powers have been attributed to garlic over the centuries. The Egyptians believed that garlic gave strength, and fed it to the workers who constructed the great pyramids. The Roman upper class did not care much for the smell of garlic, but supplied it to their soldiers to eat, believing it would give them strength and courage in battle.

As for the mystical stuff, I guess there are more stories connected with garlic than any other food item. In some parts of the world, it is still believed that garlic can ward off evil spirits. In New Orleans, if you go into one of the voodoo shops on Bourbon Street, you'll see several potions and recipes that use garlic to fight evil spirits.

There is some validity to the curative powers of garlic. In fact, in 1959 the Food and Drug Research Laboratory issued a statement proclaiming that garlic does have the ability to remove toxins from the body, which, among other things, helps to reduce blood pressure.

AVAILABLE
year-round

For peeling garlic, it's a smack! Simply place cloves on a cutting board and smack then with the bottom of a pan. The skin will lift right off.

Mystic and curative powers have been attributed to garlic over the centuries.

There are basically three types of garlic. First is the **Creole** variety, and I'm sure you know where in the States this one is most popular. Creole garlic has the strongest flavor and smell. The skin color is totally white, and it may be marketed under the name American garlic. Next is the **Italian,** sometimes called the Mexican variety. You will know this type by the purplish skin color. The Italian garlic has a nice, mild flavor. Last is the **Tahitian** variety. It's the biggest of the three basic varieties—two to three inches in diameter—and has more, but smaller, cloves. Recently, through cross-breeding, an **Elephant** variety was introduced. It has the totally white skin of the Creole and the mild flavor of the Italian, yet it is twice the size of the Tahitian variety. Elephant garlic is excellent for baking, and its divided cloves are much easier to work with because of their enormous size.

There's no need to peel the garlic if using a garlic press. The grate in the press will catch the skin for you.

Garlic is available year-round. When shopping, avoid softness, sprouting, and wetness, which are sure signs of age. Always choose firm, dry garlic with paper-like skin. If stored properly—in a paper bag placed in a cool, dry spot—garlic will keep for at least a month. Remember to keep this vegetable away from foods that could pick up its smells.

Greens

Chard

To look at **Swiss Chard,** you wouldn't think that this vegetable is related to the beet, but it is. In fact, chard is the oldest member of the beet family; it just never evolved the large round roots of its younger sibling.

Chard is believed to have originated in Asia Minor, where two types were grown: light green and dark green. In other areas, such as the Near East and the Mediterranean region, a red chard grew. (Red chard is mentioned in ancient Greek writing.)

As for its name, a sixteenth-century Swiss botanist wrote a detailed report on the various types of chard, and ever since, the agricultural world has referred to the vegetable as Swiss chard.

The Swiss chard is one of our most versatile vegetables. There are two edible parts, which can be prepared in a number of ways. First, the leaf portion can be cooked the same way we Southerners cook turnip greens; unlike turnip greens, however, chard tops also make a wonderful salad. The other edible portion is the stem, which is the part consumed by most Americans who have discovered this ancient vegetable. When fresh, the stem is beautiful in both the green and red varieties. On the green variety, the stem is a milky white color, and the texture is crisp, like celery. For the red type, the texture is the same, but the color is a cross between apple red and sunset orange.

A note for you caterers: chard stems are excellent for your *plat de crudité* (raw vegetable platter). When served raw, chard has a beet-like flavor, but when steamed, the flavor is like that of celery.

Like the beet, chard is loaded with nutrients. It's high in vitamin A and contains large amounts of potassium and iron. As for calories, one cup of chard contains only about thirty.

AVAILABLE
year-round

When de-sanding greens, use warm water to make the job much easier, especially when washing spinach.

Remember 1-1/2 pounds of spinach cooks down to about a cup.

Swiss chard is available year-round. When shopping for it, choose bunches that are high in color—deep green in the green variety and rich, bold red in the red variety. The stems should be firm but not dried out, with no darkening at the bottom. Chard should be bought no more than three days before using. Store wrapped in a damp paper towel in the refrigerator.

Collards

AVAILABLE
year-round

Those of us born in the South have been familiar with this produce item ever since we were old enough to sit down for Sunday dinner. Collards are a non-head-forming member of the cabbage family, like kale. In fact, some experts say the only difference between the two is the curly leaves, although Southerners know better. Cooked kale is a fantastic dish, but it just does not compare to the flavor and body of properly prepared collard greens.

Greens represent money. Eating them on New Year's Eve will guarantee that you have money throughout the year.

This plant has been around since prehistoric times, and it is believed to have originated in Asia, where wild collards reportedly still flourish. They were brought to this country during the fifteenth century and soon became a very popular winter vegetable because the cold seems to bring out the best flavor of the greens. Through the years their popularity has declined considerably in the North, but in the South they are just as popular as they were one hundred years ago. In fact, this region leads the nation in production and consumption of fresh collard greens.

Collards are available virtually year-round; however, those with the best flavor are on the market during fall and winter. When shopping, choose vegetables rich in color (dark green) with firm stems. Avoid any greens with wilting or yellowing leaves. Like the other members of the cabbage family, collards are extremely nutritious. Large amounts of vitamin A and riboflavin are found within the dark green leaves.

PESTO WITH A SOUTHERN BITE

In a food processor, chop first four ingredients. To this mixture add olive oil, cheese, salt, and pepper. Pesto can be served as is over noodles, chicken, and fish, or heated in a frying pan and poured over food items.

1-1/2 to 2 cups
  basil leaves
1-1/2 to 2 cups
  collard greens
3 cloves garlic
2 oz. parsley
3/4 cup olive oil
1 cup grated
  Italian cheese
salt and pepper
  to taste

Dandelion Greens

That's right. The green leaves from those little yellow flowers are edible, and, I might add, quite good. This member of the chicory family proves that one person's flower or weed is another person's gourmet salad—and it makes a nice cooked side dish, too. The first time I tried dandelion greens was in New York City. The gourmet shop I worked at carried them, and they sold very well. I remember asking Charlie Balducci, "What's the story with dandelion greens?" After he explained the culinary appeal of the weed, I took them home and, to my surprise, I totally enjoyed them.

AVAILABLE
year-round

Here is a little tip about cooking dandelion greens: Some people think that they are quite bitter, so when you cook them, pour the first water off and cook them again. I think you will find they make a great substitute for spinach.

Dandelion greens are at their flavorful best during spring and early summer. When shopping, always choose rich, green leaves with no evident wilting or yellowing. Dandelions are very nutritious. They are loaded with vitamin A, carbohydrates, calcium, and large amounts of riboflavin.

Kale

AVAILABLE
year-round

Today the primary use for this leafy vegetable is ornamental. American restaurants use this hearty, non-head-forming member of the cabbage family to decorate salad bars and fruit trays, and as garnish on serving plates. However, kale makes an excellent cooked vegetable, and its cultivation dates back so many centuries that its exact origin is unclear. It could be the Mediterranean region or Asia Minor. The ancient Greeks farmed kale, as did the Romans and, later on, the French, who introduced it to the British. By the end of the fifteenth century, kale was being grown in the New World and has been a steady crop in the United States since that time. The only greens I enjoy more when cooked in the traditional southern style are collards. If you don't know how to cook kale, any recipe you have for collards, turnips, or other greens will do.

There are two main varieties of kale: the **Scotch** and the **Blue.** They are equal in flavor and nutritional value, but the Blue is a special favorite of restaurants because of its colorful tint.

Kale is available year-round, like the other members of the cabbage family. When shopping, choose fresh-looking bunches. Be sure that the stemmed ends are clean, with no darkness, and that the leaves are fresh, with no wilting or yellowish color. As for nutritional value, kale is loaded with vitamins A, B, and C. There are also generous amounts of riboflavin, calcium, iron, and phosphorus contained in the luscious green and blue leaves of this vegetable.

Mustard Greens

This vegetable looks similar to kale but is a little more delicate. It has a lighter green color, and the stems aren't as thick. Growing up in Conyers, Georgia, we had mustard greens in the garden every year, and Mama always cooked them with turnip greens.

AVAILABLE
year-round

In the South, mustard greens are a big item, but they just aren't as popular elsewhere in the country, although the wild mustard growing in northern California looks quite tasty—and when it goes to seed, the hills come alive with blazing yellow.

DOMESTIC PEAK
fall-early winter

Mustard greens are usually at their best during fall and early winter. When shopping for them, choose leaves with a nice green color, with no wilting or yellowing.

As with all greens, try to use them the day you buy them. They will keep one or two days in a paper bag under refrigeration. If the greens are limp, plunge them into cold water for about an hour before preparing.

Mustard greens are extremely high in vitamins A and C. They're loaded with calcium and potassium and are a good source for iron.

Turnip Greens

Turnips are believed to have originated in Russia, which makes sense because they do thrive in the cooler climates. However, they have a long history of cultivation in parts of Europe (as food for people and as feed for livestock). Turnips made their appearance in North America during the mid-sixteenth century and have thrived ever since, especially in the South.

AVAILABLE
year-round

Turnip greens are not a separate vegetable, but an extension of the turnip roots, although many Americans buy them separately.

When shopping for the greens, avoid any with yellowing or wilting leaves. After purchasing, store no more than two to three days in the refrigerator in a paper bag. To revive the greens before cooking, plunge them into cold water. Traditionally, Southerners cook their turnip greens with pork, but I think they taste much better if you substitute a chicken leg or back for the pork.

When turnip roots and greens are prepared together, there are very few vegetables that can equal their nutritional punch. Vitamins A, B, C, E, and K are all present in this very nourishing dish.

Jerusalem Artichokes

AVAILABLE
year-round

**DOMESTIC
PEAK**
autumn

The name "Jerusalem artichoke" is very misleading—the vegetable has no ties to Jerusalem, and it is not in the same botanical family as the artichoke, although the cooked flavor does bring to mind (or tastebuds) the taste of cooked artichokes. A few years ago, someone decided to rename this vegetable "sunchoke" because it is actually the tuber produced underground by a type of sunflower plant.

This choke is one of the few vegetables that is native to North America, and it was a favorite of the Native Americans. On first sight, you might mistake Jerusalem artichokes for small Irish potatoes, and, in fact, the Indians used this vegetable in much the same way the Irish used the potato. Beneath the tan skin is a clean, crisp, white flesh and a nutty flavor similar to that of the Globe artichoke. But unlike that artichoke, sunchokes can be eaten raw.

Jerusalem artichokes or sunchokes—whatever they are called where you shop—are available most of the year, but they are at their peak during the fall and winter. Choose sunchokes light in color that are firm to the touch and have no mold or decay. This vegetable is an excellent source of vitamin B and iron.

Jicama

The exact origin of this vegetable is unclear; it grows wild in all the tropical zones of the world. Whereas in America the potato is king, jicama wears the crown in the tropics.

Like the potato, the jicama is also the swollen root of a vine related to the morning glory family, and the flavors of potatoes and jicamas are somewhat alike. However, the jicama contains much more water, and the average jicama sold in American produce markets is about the size of a small cantaloupe. The skin is a dark cardboard color, but inside you'll find beautiful white flesh that is crisp and crunchy.

Unlike potatoes, jicamas are great raw. I love to use it in salads, and it is also wonderful when cut into sticks and served with dips. Jicama is the perfect substitute for expensive fresh water chestnuts. Keep in mind that it may be used in any recipe that calls for potatoes. You can boil it, bake it, and even fry it. You must try this marvelous tropical vegetable; I know you will love it.

Jicamas are available year-round in produce markets and the everyday grocery store, but this tropical treasure is at its tasteful best during our fall and winter. When shopping, avoid jicamas with bruises or deep cuts. The vegetable will store uncut for weeks in the refrigerator. There is no need to bag it, but once cut, it should be used as soon as possible.

The jicama contains a fair amount of vitamin C and is loaded with potassium, yet remains low in calories, about forty-five per eight ounces.

AVAILABLE
year-round

DOMESTIC PEAK
fall-winter

Kohlrabi

AVAILABLE
year-round

In German the word *kohl* means "cabbage," and *rabi* means "turnip." Whereas most vegetables can be traced back to ancient times, the kohlrabi did not make its debut until the fifteenth century. It originated in northern Europe and by century's end was being enjoyed throughout the continent.

The kohlrabi was introduced to America in the early 1800s, and, unfortunately, the vegetable has yet to gain the popularity it deserves. Kohlrabi looks like a root vegetable, but unlike root vegetables, whose globe portions grow underground, the kohlrabi globe forms and grows above ground. This round globe reminds me of an onion, though it's a different color.

In Europe there are many varieties of kolhrabi, but only two types are cultivated in America: **Early Vienna,** which is a light green color, and **Early Purple Vienna,** whose color is like that of a fresh beet.

If you enjoy the taste of fresh turnips and the greens, but you can't handle too much of them at one time, the kohlrabi could be your answer. When cooked, kohlrabi has a mild turnip flavor. I'm sure if more Southerners would give this vegetable a try, its popularity would soar.

Kohlrabi has two edible parts. First, there is the green leafy portion, which can be cut off and cooked like spinach or other leaf vegetables. The second edible portion is the globe, whose culinary options are endless. It can be boiled, as we do root vegetables, steamed the way you would prepare broccoli, or, to make an elegant dish, cored and used in any stuffed mushroom recipe. Raw kohlrabi is as enjoyable as cooked, for it is crisp and juicy; try adding some to your next tossed salad. The purple kohlrabi is like having several vegetables in one, for not only can you cook both parts of the vegetable as suggested above, but the leaf portion also adds beautiful color to any decorative tray.

When shopping, choose young kohlrabi (size is the key; the globe should be not larger than two-and-one-half inches, about the size of a kiwi) that is fresh and full of color. Avoid kohlrabi with yellow and wilting leaves. Never choose kohlrabi whose globes are too large, for they can be tough and stringy.

Kohlrabi is high in vitamin C, and the leaf portion contains large amounts of vitamin A. The kohlrabi is also an excellent blood cleanser and contains high amounts of calcium.

Lettuce

Lettuce is believed to have first been cultivated in Asia Minor, and by the sixteenth century it was a common vegetable throughout Europe. On our continent, lettuce was one of the first vegetables planted by the early settlers, if not the very first. Nowadays lettuce, which has several varieties, rivals the potato for the number-one spot in annual American vegetable sales and consumption. At least one variety of lettuce is grown in every state in the union, including Alaska and Hawaii. In fact, I tasted the best leaf lettuce of my life while visiting the island of Maui. It was grown in the same area that is famous for the Maui sweet onion—kula—just at the foot of the dormant volcano Haleakala.

AVAILABLE
year-round

As I said, one can find lettuce growing in every state. However, the majority of the commercially grown crops (more than 75 percent) is produced by California and Arizona. California is by far the largest single producer and, in my opinion, the producer of the world's best commercially grown lettuces. Arizona is a good second.

This is not to snub the other production areas, but Salinas, California (an area just south of San Jose), has warm days and cool nights, which is perfect for lettuce. In other commercial production areas such as Florida, Texas, and New Jersey, the nights are sometimes as hot as the days, and the lettuce just is not as crisp and sweet as in California. However, I must say that over the past few years, I have noticed much improvement in those eastern lettuces.

There are dozens of varieties of lettuce, but only a few are grown commercially. First, there is crisp head lettuce—known to most consumers as **Iceberg** lettuce. The name "Iceberg" came from the way the lettuce used to be packed in the field for shipping. The vegetable was cut and trimmed, placed in a crate with a layer of ice on top, then a layer of lettuce, and so on until the crate was full. This made for a pretty heavy crate, thus the name Iceberg. Crisp head lettuce is by far the most popular salad green in America, although, in my opinion, it is far from the most tasty.

Trendy **Romaine** lettuce is considered a head lettuce, although the leaves do not close together in a round ball; rather, they close long and flat. The outer leaves of romaine are a bold, dark green, while the inner leaves are a much lighter color and are sometimes even yellow. In certain restaurants, especially on the West Coast, these golden inner leaves are prepared into separate salads altogether.

Green leaf has become quite popular over the past five years. It is a beautiful, green, curly-leaf variety that really stands out in a salad mixture. In my opinion, though, the flavor is a little flat and the texture too coarse and grassy.

Red leaf lettuce is curly, like green leaf, but that is where the similarity ends. The tips are a dark, auburn-red color. Red leaf is my personal favorite; it has a soft texture and a mild, sweet taste. Red leaf not only tastes good but is quite pleasing to the eye.

Other leaf lettuces include **Boston** lettuce, also called butter leaf lettuce because of the soft, buttery flavor and texture; and **Bibb** lettuce, which the old-timers referred to as limestone lettuce, according to Vick Korfhage of Korfhage Greenhouses in Louisville, Kentucky. Vick explains that Bibb lettuce grown in the limestone-laden fields of Kentucky has a distinct flavor, and I agree. This lettuce looks like a miniature romaine, but the only thing small about it is its size—the flavor is outstanding, whether grown in Kentucky, upstate New York, or California.

Lettuce is available year-round, but as consumers know, prices do tend to run on the high side during the winter months. However, you may not realize that if you divide the price of a head of lettuce into the per-serving cost, you will find lettuce is still a good value, even in winter.

When shopping for lettuce of any variety, freshness is key. Never choose lettuce that has wilting or yellowing leaves. Another way to detect freshness is to inspect the base of the vegetable; it should always be hard and have a pale white or pinkish color. If you notice that the produce person has trimmed the base quite a bit, that, too, is a warning sign that the retailer is trying to pass off old lettuce. Lettuce can be stored up to four days in the refrigerator, but try to use it within three.

Lettuce, even Iceberg, is a good source of vitamins A, B, and some C, plus riboflavin. What may surprise you is that lettuces are also good providers of calcium and potassium.

Mushrooms

The average consumer knows mushrooms as little white, umbrella-shaped items that are excellent in salads, soups, and sauces with meats and/or other produce items. Worldwide, over two thousand varieties of mushrooms are eaten on a somewhat regular basis, and that has been going on for more than two thousand years. Egyptian kings and Roman emperors declared mushrooms off-limits to the underclass, although any Roman citizen could eat the food of the gods on holy days.

AVAILABLE
year-round

The French are credited with being the first to cultivate this culinary wonder on a commercial scale, starting in the latter part of the eighteenth century.

Mushrooms are totally fascinating to me; they're not anchored by roots, and they don't bear flowers or leaves, not even seeds. In fact, mushrooms don't belong to the vegetable family. They are part of the fungus family, the same as the lowly but useful bread mold, and yeast. Another member of the ill-sounding fungus family is the very expensive truffle.

In the United States, mushroom farming became an industry during the latter part of the nineteenth century in Pennsylvania. To this day, that state still produces about half the mushrooms sold annually in this country. In the early days, mushrooms were farmed in caves, and because they thrive in cooler temperatures, the best quality and quantity were harvested in late autumn, winter, and early spring, with supplies dropping to zero in the heat of summer. Today, mushrooms are available year-round because the caves (mushroom houses) are constructed, and winter is constantly supplied by air conditioning. Over the past few decades, the white mushroom has become the most common type. However, before World War II, I'm told, consumers only wanted the darker types; some of the old-time produce people tell me the brown varieties have an earthier flavor, and are just plain better. My favorite mushrooms are white ones that come from California.

Of the common white varieties that we find in the retail stores, about 95 percent are U.S. Number 1. This means that these mushrooms are of uniform shape, are disease-free, and have caps closed tightly around the stems. However, there is another grade— U.S. Number 2. In the produce business we call these mushrooms "mature." Since they are a bit older than the Number 1 mushrooms, their caps are open. A large quantity of the Number 2 grade are sold by wholesalers to pizza restaurants. Because of the age, Number 2 mushrooms contain less moisture and bake more easily—and they sell at a much lower price.

Number 1 mushrooms are also divided into sizes. Button is the smallest (under one inch in diameter), then medium, large, and extra large or jumbo, which are over three inches in diameter.

The best mushrooms I ever ate came from the Petaluma Mushroom Farm, located about twenty-five miles east of Bodega Bay, California (the little town made famous in Alfred Hitchcock's movie *The Birds*). These mushrooms are just beautiful, the color is snow-white, and the shape is perfect. When I sliced into them, I was so surprised to see pink gills (gills are the inside of the mushroom covered up by the cap). Never before nor since have I seen such a pretty inside, and the flavor was outstanding. If you are out in the San Francisco Bay area, make it a point to go into a retail store and ask for mushrooms from Petaluma Mushroom Farm. They make an excellent side dish sautéed with olive oil, white wine, and minced garlic.

When shopping for white mushrooms, most experts recommend mushrooms with closed caps. I think it depends on your needs. If they're to be eaten raw or sliced into salads, choose the closed cap Number 1; but if you plan to cook with the mushrooms, the Number 2 grade mature ones do have a more distinctive flavor.

It's important to choose mushrooms that are firm, dry, and free of dark spots. It's a shame that some retailers wet their mushrooms while trying to enhance their appearance. As soon as they are taken from the cool produce section, the mushrooms start to break down and become slimy. Always avoid slimy mushrooms. Remember that mushrooms are very perishable and should be used within two or three days of purchase. If you have to store them, place the mushrooms in a paper bag before putting them in the vegetable bin. If moisture forms inside the bag, it will not fall back onto the mushrooms as easily as it would in a plastic bag.

Mushrooms are quite earthy, and thus they are a good source of iron, phosphorus, potassium, and calcium. They are low in calories and also contain small amounts of vitamins B and C.

Wild Mushrooms

These made their mark on the American gourmet scene during the '80s and are worth mentioning. In Europe, Scandinavia, and other parts of the world, gathering wild mushrooms is a common hobby, but here in the States, we have been discouraged from mushroom gathering. It takes an expert to tell whether those beautiful wild mushrooms are safe and edible or poisonous, perhaps fatal. I have had a copy of the Audubon Society's *Field Guide to North American Mushrooms* for a couple of years and explore it on regular basis, but I have never gone out into the forest to pick wild mushrooms. I guess those warnings really hit home with me. However, in the Pacific Northwest, mushroom gathering is on the rise; many people have found a large profit in their mushroom explorations. Their gatherings are air-shipped to fancy restaurants and gourmet shops across the United States and to Canada.

There are so many varieties of wild and exotic mushrooms available that you could build a store around them alone. In New York's Balducci's, the mushroom is not the centerpiece, but it is definitely a main attraction. On any given day, no less than ten varieties of cultivated and wild mushrooms are available to shoppers. On some days, as many as twenty varieties are on hand. They come from Italy, France, Oregon, and the northeastern United States, as well as Canada. Of course these mushrooms sell at above premium prices, but considering the effort that goes into the gathering, shipping, and preparing of these mushrooms, the price is worth it (and the flavors are excellent).

Here are just a few of the wild mushrooms available in gourmet shops.

The most expensive mushroom is the **Morel** (the last price I was quoted was $139.00 per pound). The color is dark gray, almost black, with a flavor that is quite earthy and very rich. The Morel looks like a natural sponge; in fact, one of its common names is the "sponge mushroom."

The ***Chantrelle*** is as pretty as its name; this variety has a deep golden yellow color, with a shape reminding me of miniature daisies. The flavor and aroma are sweet, like fresh apricots.

The ***Enoki*** is a very strange-looking mushroom—tall, very thin, off-white with miniature caps about the size of a pencil eraser. The Enoki mushrooms are excellent in salads or cooked. They look like bean sprouts.

The ***Shitake*** mushroom is native to Japan and it is as well known for the way it grows (on dead oak wood) as for the wonderful flavor it yields. There is a mushroom farm in North Carolina that has begun to produce Shitake mushrooms as good as any from the Orient. In fact, Shitakes have become a common item in American stores over the past few years, and prices have dropped dramatically.

The ***Oyster mushroom*** is still popular with pickers in the wild, but it has been domesticated over the past ten years. Oyster mushrooms grow in clusters in sawdust or other wood by-products, as well as in straw. They have an extremely wide color range, from white to gray to near black; their texture is consistent—velvety smooth. Their flavor resembles the seafood for which they were named.

There is an Oyster hybrid called ***Angel Trumpet.*** It is a clean, white mushroom. The shape is like the instrument Miles Davis played. You could say the flavor of this mushroom leaves a delightful jazz note on your palate. Other wild mushrooms to look for include the Italian ***Cremini,*** or ***Brown Field Mushroom.*** It's the parent of the white commercial mushroom. Then there is the ***Cep.*** In the Norwegian language that word means "mushroom," but the Cep I'm talking about is a large, white mushroom about the size of those old-fashioned oatmeal cookies. Another variety is the ***Porcino,*** the classic Italian mushroom. It's very difficult to find a mushroom to surpass this one's flavor and appearance. Then there is the French ***Pied du Mouton.*** This miniature golden brown mushroom is umbrella-shaped and fantastic for sautéing.

There are so many wild mushrooms out there waiting to be

discovered. If you find any, please write and share your find with me. Of course, wild mushrooms do sell for premium prices, but it doesn't take a lot of mushrooms to add a lot of flavor to your recipes.

Truffles belong to the same plant family as mushrooms—fungus. I just can't discuss mushrooms without mentioning truffles. The world's finest and most expensive truffles come from Italy's Piedmont region and the Perigord area of France. Unlike mushrooms, which spawn, then shoot upward and grow above ground, truffles grow beneath the earth. To be exact, they grow underneath the root system of small birch and oak trees. Pigs are used to gather them, and the animal is able to unearth the truffle without causing damage. Truffles are mostly used by fancy restaurants or specialty shops and do come with very high price tags.

Okra

The ancient vegetable, okra, a close relative of the cotton plant, originated in northeast Africa. I'm told it's not uncommon to see wild okra still growing today in Ethiopia and the upper Nile region.

AVAILABLE
year-round

Okra was, and still is, a staple in Africa, India, and the Mediterranean area. This unique vegetable was brought to America along with human cargo in the hulls of slave ships. Both ill-treated cargos survived harsh times in their new homeland and have made significant impacts on the culinary world.

DOMESTIC
PEAK
summer

In Africa, the words "okra" and "gumbo" are interchangeable. But in the United States, gumbo has come to mean a soup or stew associated with Creole cooking, and okra refers to the primary ingredient used in its preparation.

In my eyes, okra, with its spring-grass color and its intriguing cylindrical shape, is one of the most beautiful vegetables. I've often asked myself whether I feel this way because the history of this ancient food and my own cultural history are so closely intertwined.

I grew up eating okra, and my grandfather, W. H. Curtis, raised the best I've ever tasted. Each summer morning, he and I would inspect the plants (that looked so much like the cotton plants he spent his days with) and harvest the ripe vegetables. Then we'd take them in to my grandmother Corine, who must have had fifty different ways to prepare the fruits (vegetables) of our labor: fried, boiled, cooked with onions or tomatoes in stews, pickled, or canned. If I had known then what I would be doing for a living, I would have written down everything Gramma did in her kitchen. Thank goodness my mama knows many of Gramma's secrets.

Okra is available year-round; however, it's at its best during the hottest months of summer, July and August. When shopping, remember that big okra is not good okra; that's what my grandfather would say. Choose vegetables that are no more than three inches long and one-half inch in diameter, free from scars and wetness. The stem end, where the vegetable was cut from the plant, should have a light color; if dark, the okra is old and should be avoided.

Okra will keep up to a week in the refrigerator, stored in paper bags in the vegetable bin, but try to use it within three days of purchasing.

This prehistoric vegetable is extremely nutritious—high in vitamins A and C and a good source of potassium, iron, and calcium, yet it's low in calories.

Onions

AVAILABLE
year-round

Onions have been with us for so long that no one is exactly sure where they originated. However, records indicate that they were first raised as a crop near Asia Minor. The early Egyptians thought so highly of the power in onions that they used them not only as food but also to heal the sick. Because of its round shape, the onion was considered a symbol of eternity and of the entire universe. The Spanish explorers brought domesticated onions to the New World, and today the output of onions in the United States alone is well over two billion pounds a year. We may not think a lot about our onions, but we sure do eat them!

Onions come in all shapes and sizes, and in a few different colors. Over the last ten years, the sweet onion has really gained the market share. There are sweet onions from Georgia, Texas, California, Washington State, and Hawaii. Now, I'm not going to get into the argument as to which state produces the sweetest onion—but remember, I'm from Georgia. Among the red sweet onions are the **Italian Red** and the **Red Torpedo** (also called Bottle onions because they have a long, cylindrical shape). One key tip to remember when buying onions: the flatter the onion, the milder the taste.

For no more tears, my daughter gave me a great tip for cutting onions: put on your sun glasses. The shades keep the onion vapors from reaching your eyes. It works!

I guess the round onions are the most popular when it comes to cooking. They are also the strongest as far as flavor is concerned—so they're the ones that will make you cry when you're cutting them up. This type can be either red, yellow, or white.

As for the small onions, the ones you see in the store labeled "pearl onions" or "green onions" could be any variety that was harvested before reaching full maturity. Therefore, pearl onions can be any of the three colors—red, white, or yellow. Green onions have green tops and white bottoms (see the description of green onions for more information).

Onions are available year-round, either fresh or from storage, and the price varies little. Look for the best sweet onions during spring and early summer.

When shopping for onions, avoid onions that have sprouted; they're too old. Look for firm onions with no soft spots. The skin should be dry and should peel off easily. Make sure there is no dampness at the top or bottom of the vegetable.

For peeling small onions: boil them about 2 minutes, then cut off the root and squeeze from the opposite end. The skin will slip right off.

Scallions

Let's clear up two misconceptions at the outset. First, scallions and green onions are not different types of onions; they are one and the same. Second, no, this thick, grassy-looking vegetable is not a miniature variety of onion. Scallions are young onion plants of any variety that have been harvested before reaching full maturity, usually before the white bulbs reach half an inch in diameter.

AVAILABLE
year-round

Whether you call them scallions or green onions depends on which part of the country you are from. Below the Mason-Dixon Line and to the west Texas state line, they're called green onions (except in New Orleans, of course; those Cajuns and Creoles love French-sounding names).

According to most experts, the best are grown in California, New Jersey, or the Ohio Valley. To that I say, "What do they have against the South?" I have eaten scallions from these states, which all produce excellent crops, and California does lead the nation in production of this little vegetable, but in my opinion, the best come from Georgia. Down in south Georgia, the farmers have started to harvest Vidalia green onions during spring, and everyone knows how good Vidalias are.

When you shop for scallions (green onions), let appearance be your guide. If the tops are nice and green and the bottoms are white and clean, you've got a winner. Also keep in mind that 99 percent of this vegetable is edible. We Americans usually disregard those delightful green tops. If you fall into that group, stop; the tops add fantastic flavors to just about anything. When cooking rice or steaming other vegetables, add chopped scallions for a new twist. Add them to beef stew or fried pork chops and chicken, and don't forget scallions are wonderful for garnishing soups and salads.

This little vegetable may not be the most nutritious item in the produce section, but it does contain fair amounts of protein, carbohydrates, and calcium. Available year-round, scallions sell for moderate prices.

Shallots

AVAILABLE
year-round

**DOMESTIC
PEAK**
*July-
October*

Shallots may very well be the most interesting type of onion, for this little beauty takes on characteristics from every other member of the onion family. The size is about the same as that of the little green scallion; yet the skin color is a rusty brown, like that of the fully matured Spanish onion. Lastly, the shallot is divided into cloves like its other cousin, garlic. As for flavor, it's not as pungent as garlic, but it adds more zest than the normal Spanish onion to which we are accustomed.

The shallot was first introduced to the United States during the middle of the sixteenth century by the Spanish explorer Hernando de Soto. This vegetable was very popular in the Louisiana Territory, and it still is in that part of the country. Shallots were once a major cash crop for Louisiana, which produced well in excess of ten million pounds annually. Unfortunately for Louisiana farmers, as the less expensive scallion gained popularity, shallot sales dropped nearly to nothing.

Today, with the spread of gourmet cooking, shallots, which at times bring prices ten times greater than scallions, are making a significant comeback. There are some commercial growers in California, New York, and other parts of the United States, including Louisiana. However, the majority of fresh shallots come to American consumers from Europe, with France being the biggest and best supplier of this gourmet item.

Shallots are available pretty much year-round, although new crops of shallots are available July through October. During other months, they come from storage. As for which is best, fresh or seasoned, many professional chefs swear there are no onions as flavorful as fresh shallots, but an equal number of chefs claim shallots should be seasoned to reach their peak flavor. I have no personal preference.

When shopping, choose shallots less than one inch in diameter unless they are specified as jumbo, which of course are much larger. Although they are easier to handle and work with, jumbo shallots just don't have the flavor of the smaller type. The shallots should be firm, and the skin should be smooth and dry. Avoid shallots in which sprouting has occurred, for sprouting is a sure sign of age or improper storage. At home, if stored properly—closed tightly in a brown paper bag and placed in a cool, dark location—shallots will keep for weeks.

Like other members of the onion family, shallots contain fair amounts of vitamins A and C. However, nutrition is not as important with this vegetable because of its size. I don't think anyone would want to eat a half-pound of shallots! But I do want to reemphasize the excellent flavor it adds. When your recipe calls for onion and/or garlic, add diced shallots also. I'm sure you will love the new twist.

Oriental Vegetables

AVAILABLE
varieties,
year-round

As recently as five to ten years ago, Chinese vegetables were thought to be strange or exotic and were very hard to find outside the big-city Chinatown areas of San Francisco and New York. However, today things have changed. With the ever-increasing popularity of these items, many supermarket chains have designated large parts of their produce sections for Oriental vegetables, which taste great and are very nutritious—not to mention that they cook with relative ease in a short time, which is perfect for the America of the '90s.

Bean Sprouts. This vegetable has made it into the mainstream. Twenty years ago, you couldn't pay most people to try bean sprouts, but now they are so popular that they are not even thought of as an Oriental vegetable. I guess the majority of bean sprouts used in this country are tossed into salads, but don't forget that they're also wonderful when cooked.

CURTIS'S HOME FOO YOUNG

2 Tbl. flour
3 to 4 eggs
1/4 cup green peas
1/4 cup carrots, diced
1 bunch green onions,
   diced
1 cup bean sprouts
Vegetarian Gravy
2 tsp. olive oil

Put oil in a heavy skillet to warm. Mix all ingredients. Drop large spoonfuls of the mixture into the hot oil to form patties. Fry until brown. Serve with Vegetarian Gravy (*recipe on page 175*).

Bittermelon (*foo gwa*). This is another vegetable used quite often in soups. I guess we could call it the Chinese cucumber. It is light green with bumpy grooves up and down the surface. Inside, the flesh is white and pink and quite attractive.

Bok Choy. This vegetable, which originated in Asia, has been a mainstay for centuries throughout the Orient. It is one of my favorite Oriental vegetables. Bok choy is very similar to Swiss chard; in fact, many people confuse the two. When fresh, bok choy, like the smaller Swiss chard, has beautiful, milky white stalks with bold green leaves. Unlike Swiss chard, I don't recommend using the edible green tops of bok choy for fresh salads; when eaten raw, these greens have a hot, spicy taste that I just don't care for—and I don't know anyone else who enjoys it either. When cooked, though, the hotness seems to disappear and the tops become a nice dinner vegetable. The stalks, however, are mild and can be eaten raw, although few people do since the texture is watery and quite crunchy. When steamed or sautéed, these stalks become much more tender and sweet. Sometimes baby bok choy is available. These little jewels can be cooked whole, steamed or boiled, and I highly recommend them. Bok choy is low in calories but high in both vitamins A and C, and contains large amounts of calcium. In fact, a cup of cooked bok choy provides as much calcium as a cup of milk.

The pointers for selecting bok choy are similar to those for selecting Swiss chard. Choose vegetables with good color and no darks spots. I recommend buying bok choy no more than three days prior to using. Wrap the vegetable in a damp paper towel and store in your refrigerator.

Chinese Long Bean (*dow kok*). The first time I saw this vegetable I was in the San Francisco Golden Gate Produce Terminal. I had no idea what it was. It looked like green pieces of rope, scrap pieces at that, about one foot long and about a quarter-inch in diameter. But I found that when cooked, these green beans are very tasty and tender, similar to the French *haricots verts*.

Chinese Mustard Green (*kai choy*). The bitterness is slightly stronger than that of the mustard green found in the American South. In Chinese cuisine it is most often featured in soups or as a stir-fry ingredient.

Chinese Okra (*sing gwa*). This vegetable could be called giant okra, as it is eight to twelve inches long and about an inch thick. The color is much deeper than we Southerners are accustomed to seeing in our little okra, but its flavor reminds me of our own backyard okra.

Chinese Snow Pea, or ***Chinese Pea Pod.*** This is another of the Oriental vegetables that has worked its way into the American mainstream, and the only reason young Americans know of its Oriental origin is because of its name. Snow peas are by far the most popular of the Oriental vegetables. They're great raw or cooked, and mix well with meat, fish, and other vegetables. Fresh steamed snow peas and sliced carrots makes an elegant dish; sautéed snow peas in white wine and butter are also fantastic.

The snow pea has a flat pod, unlike the English pea, and whereas the round, glossy green pod of English peas is inedible, the flat, light green pods of snow peas are sweet and tender. Most people think the biggest difference between the snow pea and English pea is the price; English peas may sell for one dollar per pound and snow peas at two dollars per pound. However, keep in mind that from the one pound of snow peas you purchased, you can cook and serve at least 95 percent of them. We never get that much yield from English peas.

When purchasing snow peas, select none longer than three inches since longer peas tend to be stringy. Choose peas that are light green in color and firm to the touch. Never take peas that show a yellowish color and have dry ends, for they are past their peak and just do not have the sweetness of young tender peas.

Chinese Squash (*mo qua*). I hate to say it, but I still have yet to acquire a taste for this vegetable. Maybe it is because of the fuzzy skin. They are light green and resemble zucchini, except that they have fuzzy skin and are about six inches long.

Daikon (*low bok*). This giant white radish is about twice the size of a large carrot. The Japanese truly love this vegetable. In fact, it is the number one crop in Japan, where it is very rare to be served a rice dish without daikon. The texture and taste are similar to red radish, but not quite as hot.

Ginger Root. Most consumers don't think of it as Oriental, but it is. This brown-skinned beauty has worked its way into many American kitchens. The dry powdered and crystal forms of ginger found in the grocery section of the supermarket just can't stand up when compared to fresh ginger. Fresh ginger is imported from many tropical zones, including the Fiji Islands, but the best comes from Hawaii. It is available year-round, and when stored properly, will last for weeks in the refrigerator wrapped tightly in plastic or paper bags. Fresh ginger is extremely versatile and easy to work with. Peel it first, then add very thin slices to salads or use it in a stir-fry or with just about any marinade. Next time you are at a supermarket and need ginger, try the fresh stuff first.

Tofu. This item may not be as popular as snow peas or bean sprouts, but it is just as famous and maybe more so. Tofu is the perfect food, some say, and an excellent meat substitute for vegetarians, being extremely high in protein. Tofu is not really a vegetable; rather, it is a by-product of ground soybeans that have been soaked, allowed to transform into a semisolid mass, and then pressed to remove excess moisture. When the process is finished, the result is something that looks very much like cheese, and in fact it should be stored in the same manner. I'm not the biggest tofu fan, but I do enjoy it when cooked into Chinese foods or other Oriental dishes.

Wintermelon (*dong qua*). On first sight one might mistake it for a little watermelon, but inside, the flesh is solid white and not sweet at all. Wintermelons are extremely tasty, though, when cooked into fish or shrimp dishes.

Parsnips

AVAILABLE
year-round

**DOMESTIC
PEAK**
*October-
February*

Like many old European vegetables, this one was brought to America by the early settlers. It looks just like its relative the carrot, with the exception of color; parsnips are off-white. The parsnip is believed to have originated in the Mediterranean region. By the mid-sixteenth century, this vegetable had established itself as quite an important cash crop, or should I say a survival crop for the poor and underprivileged of that time throughout Germany.

I guess I should tell you that the parsnip is not one of my favorite vegetables, but I do enjoy it on occasion, especially if the vegetable has been left in the ground until after at least one cold spell. Cold weather allows the starch in this rather bitter vegetable to convert to sugar, which makes it pleasantly sweet (not as sweet as a carrot) and nutty. Therefore, I find the best parsnips from October through February.

When selecting parsnips, choose small to medium vegetables that are free from scars and damage. If stored properly parsnips will keep in your refrigerator for up to seven days in a paper bag. This vegetable contains small amounts of vitamin A. It also contains vitamin C and various other minerals. Since parsnips are related to carrots, they may be substituted in recipes that call for carrots.

Peppers

Peppers, like their botanical cousins, tomatoes, are native to the New World. However, after Columbus introduced them to Europe, the vegetable became popular, and spread rapidly throughout the Far East. In fact, hot peppers are cultivated and consumed in such large quantities in India that they are often believed to have originated there.

There are far too many pepper varieties to list them all, but basically there are only two types—hot and sweet. How do you tell the two apart? You could bite into them, but you may pay the price with a red tongue, so remember this: the bigger the pepper, the milder or sweeter the taste; the smaller the pepper, the hotter the pop.

Two of the hot peppers, also known as chiles, are the **Anaheim,** which is considered the mildest of the hot peppers, and the **Pasilla**—also called Poblano or Ancho—which has greenish-black skin and is heart-shaped.

Now for the hot-hot chiles: First is the **Fresno,** which is light green, about one to two inches long, and has a rather pointed end. Next is one of the world's most popular peppers, the **jalapeño,** which is dark green and has somewhat of a cylindrical shape. The hottest of all chiles is the **Serrano;** the best way to describe it would be to say it is a miniature jalapeño, but hotter. The Serrano will light you up!

Among the sweet peppers, the most popular are the **Bells, Green** and **Red;** they are the same variety of pepper, but the red ones have been left on the vine long enough to reach full maturity. As the green bell pepper ripens, the color changes and the flavor becomes sweeter. There are also **Yellow, Orange,** and **Purple Bells,** which all start as green. If you would like to break away from the bell and try other sweet peppers, I recommend **Cubanelles,** also known in the South as banana peppers or Italian frying peppers.

AVAILABLE
year-round

DOMESTIC PEAK
August-September

They are excellent when sautéed with other vegetables.

All the varieties of peppers are great sources of vitamin C and are low in calories. The red bell peppers are also a good source of vitamin A.

Fresh peppers are available year-round, with the season peaking August through September. When shopping, choose peppers high in color and free of bruises, scars, and wrinkles. All are signs of age. Uncut fresh peppers placed in a paper bag can be stored in the refrigerator about seven days. Once cut, they should be used within three days for the best flavor.

Potatoes

AVAILABLE
year-round

To Bake Potatoes:
If you want a true
baked potato,
don't wrap it in
foil. Foil traps
moisture, and you
end up with a
steamed potato.
Potatoes baked
without the foil
are dry cooked,
and the end
product
is fluffier.

People think potatoes originated in Ireland, but the potato actually got its start in South America and was brought to Europe by Spanish explorers. In the eighteenth century, settlers from Ireland brought potatoes to North America, so this vegetable became known as the Irish potato.

The potato is the world's largest-selling fresh vegetable. There is only one crop of potatoes per year, but they are harvested in one region or another three out of the four seasons. Therefore, the supply is uninterrupted year-round. The potatoes dug in the fall are usually put in storage. These are best for frying, mashing, and baking because they don't contain as much moisture as the fresh potatoes that are dug in spring and summer. In the produce business, potatoes harvested in fall are referred to as "old" potatoes.

Often thought to be red-skinned, new potatoes can be white or red. Potatoes harvested and sold in spring and summer are classified as "new potatoes." Fresh potatoes, because of the moisture, don't fry well and take a very long time to bake, but when boiled, they are fantastic.

All red-skinned potatoes are not new potatoes. In the Dakotas and parts of Minnesota, they grow a potato called **Red Bliss.** This potato is harvested in the fall and put into storage. Most of the Red Bliss potatoes, by the time they are ready to ship to market, have dried out and have been colored with food coloring to enhance their appearance. Most shoppers mistake these for new potatoes. So remember, the Red Bliss potato you see in wintertime is an old potato, so you would save a lot of money if you went ahead and bought the white-skinned potato during winter. For the record, new potatoes that are grown in Florida, California, Arizona, and Texas start to come to market in February. But to be sure the potatoes you are buying are new potatoes, ask your produce person.

Potatoes come in two different shapes: round, which grow mainly east of the Mississippi, and long, grown in the west. In California, they grow clear-skinned potatoes named **White Rose;** this is a new potato, but these large white potatoes make good bakers. The other potato grown out west has a brown-colored skin and is named **Russet.** This potato grows very well in northern California, Oregon, and Washington. When you put the name "Idaho" in front of a potato, most people think it's a totally different potato, but it's still a Russet. The Russet potato is the nation's largest-selling potato. In Idaho they do seem to grow bigger and cleaner. The Russets grown in Idaho also seem to cook better than Russets grown in other areas.

What is the best potato? No, it's not the Russet. The **Finnish** potatoes, I think, are by far the best all-purpose potatoes available. The flesh is yellow, and they look fantastic and taste wonderful. When I bake this potato, I don't use butter or salt—just the natural flavor is enough. This type of potato is relatively new in the marketplace, so please look for it. I'm sure you'll grow to love it as much as I do. Remember, it's Finnish potatoes.

Potatoes are rich in potassium and vitamin C (if unpeeled), and are naturally low in sodium and fat. One large potato contains about 135 calories. Choose potatoes that are clean and smooth and very firm. Always store potatoes in a cool, dry area with good air circulation.

To Boil Potatoes: For mashing or making potato salad, boiling the potatoes in vegetable broth will give your final dish more flavor.

To speed up baking time, push a metal skewer through each potato. The skewer becomes a heat conductor. In fact you can push a long skewer through three potatoes, leaving about an inch between them. This not only speeds the baking, but also gives you a handle to take the potatoes out of the oven.

Radishes

This little vegetable has been around for thousands of years. (Maybe I shouldn't say "little," because there are some members of the radish family that are much bigger than the carrot—see daikon in the Oriental vegetables section.) The radish is believed to have originated in the Orient, and it comes in various shapes, sizes, and colors. The most common type in the U.S. is the red radish.

The black radish looks like a big, dark beet with wrinkly, soft-looking skin, or—perhaps a better description for you Southerners— like a black walnut just before it falls from the tree. Beneath the skin is a white, crisp flesh with a snappy taste. Black radishes are very popular in Eastern Europe; there, the vegetable is sliced paper thin, then chilled, and served with dark bread and chicken fat. I don't have a recipe, so if you or an ancestor of yours is Eastern European, send me your recipe! I promise to put it in my next book.

Another type of radish is the icicle. Guess what color it is? No, it's not clear; it's snow white. The icicle radish is a long, skinny radish, sold in retail stores in package bags. The texture is about the same as that of the red and black types; however, it has a zestier or hotter taste.

But the icicle radish is not the hottest type. That title belongs to the biggest member of the family: the horseradish, which is also the ugliest radish! Not too many of us use fresh horseradish because of the preparation involved. It's too hard to cut with a knife, and when you do get it cut or peeled, it has to be grated. It's much easier to go to the dairy department and buy a jar. If you do that for this item, I wouldn't blame you—though freshly grated horseradish and vinegar makes a nice paste.

Radishes are available all year. I think it's safe to say that you needn't worry about a shortage.

The red radish (which, as I say, is the most common type in the U.S.) is sold two ways: in fresh bunches with the green tops attached or trimmed (and not so fresh) in small plastic bags. The fresh radish usually brings a higher price than its bagged counterpart. When I can choose between fresh or bagged radishes, I pay the higher price and buy the fresh ones, because one never knows how long the bag has been sitting in some refrigerator, either in the store or in a warehouse.

When shopping for fresh radishes, check the green tops; if they're nice and fresh, you have a winner. Make sure there is no wilting, and avoid slimy leaves. If the tops have been trimmed and the vegetable just laid out without the tops, ask for a better price. If you choose bagged radishes, pick them up and give them a feel; if they are soft and spongy, they're too old; don't buy them. If the radish is firm, it's fresh.

As with carrots, once you select fresh radishes, remove the green tops. If left attached, the tops draw moisture from the vegetable, causing it to become dry, woody, and tasteless. In other parts of the world the green tops are used as cooked vegetables or are served, fresh and raw, in salads. If you try this, please let me know what you think.

After removing the green tops (or emptying the radishes from their bag) place them in the refrigerator for up to a week. Try to use them earlier.

This vegetable isn't usually consumed in very large amounts, so keep that in mind when considering the following nutritional information: the radish is low in calories, contains good amounts of vitamins C and A, and is high in calcium and potassium.

Rhubarb

AVAILABLE
year-round

DOMESTIC PEAK
January-September

In some parts of the country this vegetable (yes, rhubarb is a vegetable, although most people think it is a fruit because of its use in desserts) is known as pie plant.

The rhubarb has quite a medical history. In colonial days, the rhubarb was thought to be a cure for tired blood; in its homeland of China, in ancient times, it was used primarily for its healing values. Nowadays, the only thing it heals is a sweet tooth.

There are two types of rhubarb available for retail consumption: field-grown and hot house. The season for field-grown rhubarb begins in spring and winds down in the fall. In this crop, the stalks are often more green than red, with very large green leaves. The texture is coarse and quite stringy. As for flavor, it is very tart and requires lots of sugar in preparation.

The hot house type ("cultivated," as the producers like to say) begins its season in January and ends in mid-summer; California and Michigan are among the leading suppliers. The color is like that of a nice rosé wine, almost pink, with leaves that are sometimes bright yellow and quite pleasant to the eye. The texture is much less coarse and stringy compared to its outdoor counterpart, as well as being less tart in flavor, therefore requiring much less sugar during preparation.

Rhubarb is available most of the year, but supplies are limited during November and December. When shopping, choose firm, erect stalks. If leaves are attached, avoid any with wilting or dark spots. This vegetable is extremely perishable, so it should be used as soon as possible after purchase. If you have to store it, keep it refrigerated in a paper bag.

Rhubarb is very high in potassium. A good source for calcium and phosphorus, it also provides some of vitamins A and C.

Spinach

Spinach originated in Persia and is now quite popular the world over—except with me when I was a kid. Back then, I wouldn't touch the stuff—I didn't care how strong it made Popeye. Now I find it's not so bad, especially in salad with my ex-wife's poppy seed dressing. Hey! Popeye ate that canned stuff—so I was right then, and I'm right now: if you have a choice between fresh or canned spinach, go with the fresh. It tastes better.

AVAILABLE
year-round

DOMESTIC PEAK
spring

There are two types of spinach: smooth, which until about ten or fifteen years ago was used mostly for processing, and curly, which was mostly sold fresh. Nowadays, the opposite is true, although on the East Coast, the curly type is still very popular.

Over the last few years the spinach folks have been marketing prewashed spinach, packaged in a cellophane bag. This prepackaged spinach is catching on. In fact, my ex-wife never allowed me to bring bunch spinach home; it's too much work to clean, she said (and she was right).

There is no difference in taste or nutritional content between smooth and curly spinach, but if you have a choice between the two, go with the smooth. The curly type has much bigger stems; that cuts down on your yield, and it takes quite a bit of fresh spinach for a serving.

Spinach is available year-round, with the season peaking during the spring and dropping to its low during the hot months of summer.

When shopping for spinach, try to buy it the day you plan to use it, even if you're buying the prewashed, bagged kind. Choose bunches that have a fresh look—no wilting or yellow leaves—and that have not been trimmed. Inspect the bagged spinach well and ask the produce person when the spinach arrived; if it's been in the store more than three days, pass on it and ask when the next supply is expected.

Again, try to use spinach the day you buy it. If you must store it, place it in a paper bag in the refrigerator for no more than two days.

Spinach is loaded with vitamins A, B, and C. It's low in fat and calories and is a great source for iron, calcium, phosphorous, and potassium.

Squash

Summer Squash

AVAILABLE
varieties,
year-round

Zucchini, yellow, and the **white patty pan** are all members of the group that for centuries has been called summer squash. These vegetables are native to the Americas, so by the time the first European settlers arrived, the squash was well established. In fact, "askootasquash" was a staple for the Native Americans. The settlers dropped the first part of the Indian word to derive the term "squash."

In the past, these squashes were available only during the warmer months of the year, and since the season peaks during summer, were labeled "summer" squash. Today, with improved varieties, better agricultural techniques, and refrigeration, zucchini, yellow, and patty pan are in season year-round, so the name summer squash may be obsolete.

This group is normally harvested before reaching full maturity, leaving the vegetables with soft, edible shells and seeds. The flesh texture is smooth, creamy, and string-free when cooked, unlike their winter counterparts. The unopened flower of these squashes is quite the gourmet item, and sometimes brings as much as fourteen dollars per pound. These squash flowers are very tasty when dipped in egg with salt and pepper, then lightly floured and sautéed.

When shopping for summer squash, freshness is most important: if fresh, the vegetable tends to be on the sweet side; if old, it becomes bitter. Size is also important; for best flavor, choose squash no more than six inches long and two inches wide—true for both zucchini and yellow squash. The patty pan should be no more than three to four inches around and one-and-a-half inches high. The squash should be firm, but not hard. Soft squash is old and should be avoided. Squash will store up to a week in the refrigerator.

Summer squash, like its winter cousins, is very nutritious, being high in vitamins A, B, and C, and also in protein, yet low in calories. The mineral value is also good; squash contains fair amounts of calcium and phosphorus and is very high in potassium.

Winter Squash

Sometimes it seems—in these days of hybrid fruits and vegetables—that the growers have forgotten the most important thing: taste! The acorn and the other types of winter squash, however, are just as flavorful today as they were a century ago.

AVAILABLE *fall- spring*

Acorn squash is also called table queen or Danish squash. It looks like an acorn nut that has large grooves, but it's about the size of a cantaloupe. Its outer skin is very hard and dark green with patches of orange. Acorn squash looks good as a table decoration and has a sweet, nutty flavor and a fibrous texture. It can be baked or steamed.

Butternut squash, another winter variety, does not have as nutty a flavor as the acorn type, but has a smooth and creamy texture. It can be baked like a sweet potato, but the most common cooking method is to boil and mash it.

Other winter squash you may want to try include **Banana** squash, which when fully mature can weigh as much as seventy pounds (most retailers sell this squash by the slice); and **sweet dumpling** squash, which looks like a miniature pumpkin and has a large seed cavity that makes it great for stuffing.

Winter squash may be the easiest squash of all to buy. All varieties of winter squash have a very hard rind, so hard that each year in the produce business, we hear of someone who has been hurt by being hit with one of these squashes. Hardness is your key. If the squash you select has any soft spots, avoid it and pick another. If you are buying a slice of squash such as Banana or **Hubert** squash, ask your produce person when the squash was cut to be sure that it has not dried out.

To cook acorn squash, cut it in half. Remember to be very careful, since this squash has a very hard rind and your knife may slip. Discard seeds—some winter squash seeds may be roasted and eaten. After squash is halved, sprinkle with brown sugar and butter, then bake at 350 degrees for 40-45 minutes.

You can also take the halves and stuff them with meat or sausage and bake it that way. Or, try acorn and butternut squash stuffed with ground turkey, mushrooms, olives, and diced onions.

Winter squashes are available starting in autumn, and the season winds down in spring. They are some of the most nutritious vegetables of all: loaded with potassium, calcium, and phosphorus and extremely high in vitamin A.

Pumpkins

Pumpkins have been grown in North America for centuries; to the American Indian, the pumpkin was very important. As food, this vegetable (which is a type of winter squash) was harvested in late autumn and would keep well into winter, when meat and other game were scarce. The Indians also used the pumpkin as pottery.

AVAILABLE
August-October

Nowadays, the pumpkin is primarily used as an ornamental item. Over 75 percent of all the pumpkins sold annually in America are purchased in October. Poor pumpkins, on November 1 no one cares about them, because during the month of October, we are all in search of that perfect, orange, spiral-shaped winter squash to transform into "Mr. Jack-O'-Lantern."

When I lived out west, every year I would go to the town of Half Moon Bay, located about sixty miles south of San Francisco, to their annual Pumpkin Festival. It was not uncommon to see pumpkins weighing over two hundred pounds.

For people in the produce business, pumpkins are the true sign of autumn. They start to show up on the market in late August. By the end of September, from the Golden Gate Produce Terminal in San Francisco to Hunt's Point Market in New York, the world of fresh vegetables is overrun by the largest and one of the tastiest of the winter squash. By November 1, they are all but gone.

There's a heck of a lot more to do with pumpkins than just make pies and Jack-O'-Lanterns. This winter squash can be steamed, stewed, roasted, sautéed, baked, or even used as serving dishes. Roasting pumpkin seeds can be a great family activity. Seeds that are roasted and salted are delicious and, especially for vegetarians, are a wonderful source of protein. Be warned, however, they also contain a good deal of fat.

Roasted Pumpkin Seeds

Wash seeds, removing all the membrane, and pat dry. Butter the baking dish liberally and spread the seeds out. Salt as desired. Bake at 400 degrees about 15 minutes.

seeds from one
Jack-O'-Lantern
butter and salt

For cooking or carving, look for a pumpkin that has a nice even shape, a long green stem, rich orange coloring, and no scars or spots. Hardness is the key.

Like the other winter squashes, the pumpkin is extremely nutritious and low in calories. It is very high in vitamin A, calcium, and potassium.

Sweet Potatoes and Yams

AVAILABLE
year-round

DOMESTIC
PEAK
August-
September

Potatoes, sweet
potatoes, and
yams should
never be stored
in the refrigerator.

Here in the United States, the terms "sweet potato" and "yams" are used interchangeably, but the two are different. Sweet potatoes are the swollen roots of a vine related to the morning glory family. I think the best-tasting ones are grown in the South. Yams, on the other hand, are actually native to the tropics and are rarely available fresh in the local grocery store.

Sweet potatoes originated in Central America, but now are grown in every subtropical climate on earth. The Portuguese took sweet potatoes to India and Malaya, and the Spaniards took them to the Indies. Explorers tried to introduce sweet potatoes to Europe; however, the climate is just too cool for their cultivation. Despite their worldwide popularity, sweet potatoes are, to this day, virtually unknown in Europe. In Asia, sweet potatoes are o popular that they are often referred to as Japanese potatoes.

There are basically two types of sweet potatoes grown in the United States. The one most people call a yam has orange-colored flesh. Over the past eight years, a red-fleshed sweet potato has increased in popularity; North Carolina and Louisiana are among the states leading production of these each year. These potatoes, when fresh, are moist and very sweet. The other sweet potato, often called Jersey sweet, has a pale yellow or whitish flesh. They are not quite as sweet as the deeper-colored potatoes, but they are still very tasty.

Sweet potatoes are available year-round, with the peak season running August through September. When shopping, remember: small to medium sweet potatoes usually have a better flavor and smoother texture. Choose firm, uniform potatoes that are free of cuts and scars. Also avoid any potato with wet spots or mold. Sweet potatoes should never be stored in the refrigerator. Always store in a cool, dry area. They will keep up to two weeks, but try to consume them sooner.

Sweet potatoes are one of our most versatile and nutritious vegetables. In fact, in many undeveloped countries, this vegetable is used as the major food staple. One medium sweet potato contains about twice the daily requirement of vitamin A and only has about 130 calories. They are also high in vitamin C and contain large amounts of iron. You can bake them, fry them, and do something else you have probably never tried: sweet potatoes are great raw, diced in a tossed salad.

Tomatoes

The tomato is technically a vegetable; in fact, it is the third most popular vegetable, ranking behind lettuce and potatoes. As popular as tomatoes are, you would think we Americans have been eating them since we stepped off the *Mayflower.* (Well, I'm sure my ancestors did not step off the *Mayflower,* but you know what I mean.) Not so. Tomatoes belong to the nightshade family, which includes some deadly fruits. For that reason, the early settlers were afraid to consume them.

AVAILABLE
year-round

Well, they finally started to eat them around 1880, and tomatoes soon became a strong cash crop, which they still are. That is when the question, "Is it a fruit or a vegetable?" came up because of trade regulations pertaining to the two different groups. In 1893, the United States Supreme Court ruled that the tomato is a vegetable.

To cut down on the acid in tomatoes when cooking, add a bit of sugar.

For the last few years, different colors and shapes of tomatoes have been making quite an impact on our market: pink, orange, pear-shaped, cherry tomatoes, and yellow ones, to name a few. I can still remember the first time I ate a yellow pear tomato. I was in a restaurant in Los Angeles, and my eyes almost jumped out of my head. The taste was wonderful. I grabbed a handful and took them out of the restaurant with me. When I got back to San Francisco, I bragged on the pretty yellow tomatoes I had eaten. Charlie Benicort, one of the most knowledgeable men on exotic produce in the United States, said to me, "Curtis, the first tomatoes grown were yellow," which was quite a surprise to me.

Now, the next time you are in one of those fancy gourmet stores—you know, like the one I dream of owning some day—and see an advertisement for "new" pear-shaped or yellow tomatoes, you'll know there is nothing new about them. It's just that we have rediscovered them.

For seeding tomatoes: cut in half and squeeze gently over a strainer, so as not to lose the juice.

When shopping for tomatoes (of any variety or shape), look for full-colored, ripe but firm vegetables that are free of bruises. By "full color," I mean red all over or, if you are buying orange tomatoes, orange from the blossom (top) end to the stem (bottom) end where the vegetable was removed from the plant. If you want to prepare one of our southern favorites, fried green tomatoes, then it's okay to buy green tomatoes. Otherwise, green or immature tomatoes just don't reach that peak flavor.

Avoid soft, spongy tomatoes for sandwiches and salads. However, those tomatoes should not be thrown out, for they are perfect for cooking in soups or sauces.

Firm tomatoes will keep unrefrigerated for about two, maybe three days before you will notice them becoming softer. At that point, it is okay to refrigerate them. If you don't consume them within two additional days, freeze them, for they will cook just as well in six months.

Tomatoes are loaded with nutrients. They're packed with calcium, phosphorus, and potassium—not to mention vitamin A. All of that, and only about twenty-five calories per medium tomato!

HERBS

In Latin, the word *herba* means "grass." *The American Heritage Dictionary* defines *herb* as "(1) a plant that has a fleshy stem as distinguished from the woody tissue of shrubs and trees, and that dies back at the end of each growing season." This is an excellent botanical definition, but the definition we garden grocers refer to is "(2) any of various often aromatic plants used especially in medicine or as seasoning." This definition almost gives a history of the plant group.

Through the ages, herbs—fresh and dried—have been prized for their aromatic value. I wouldn't be surprised if they were first used as an air freshener by some caveperson.

Herbs have also been praised for their healing powers. They have been used in medicine for thousands of years, but they have also been feared for their connection to the supernatural. If you don't believe me, check out the voodoo shops in New Orleans.

Most of all, herbs have been loved through the centuries for their ability to improve the flavor of the foods they are added to. During the Middle Ages and before refrigeration, herbs were used very heavily to cover the smell and foul taste of old meat, meat that by today's standards would be considered rotten. With better storage and cooking facilities, we've found that herbs used with a lighter hand mean better taste.

In this section, I will discuss some of the more common herbs and encourage you to make more use of them. Buy only small quantities of herbs, with fresh stems and leaves. Nothing replaces the flavor of fresh herbs, and I recommend their use whenever possible. When you must use dried herbs in the place of fresh, use only half the quantity.

As one who loves adding fresh herbs to his cooking, I have to tell you flavored oils are like having liquid herbs at your fingertips, and no stems! They take a little time to make but I enjoy doing it and I think you will too. There are two basic methods of preparation.

For chopping herbs: If it's tough for you to do on a cutting board, remove any large stems and place the herbs in a glass measuring cup. Stick your kitchen scissors in and snip vigorously until all herbs are cut to your liking.

HERB OILS

The Cold Method:

16 oz. unflavored oil

4 oz. any herb

The Cold Method, first and easiest: pour 16 ounces of unflavored oil into a container, add 4 ounces of the herb you have chosen and leave the mix undisturbed for several days in your refrigerator. When you are ready to use the oil simply strain to remove the herbs.

The Hot Method:

For faster results, the Hot Method takes a little more work but it's not difficult. Add herbs to oil and pour the mixture into a sauce pan. Heat the oil to 120 degrees. That temperature is hot enough to speed up the flavor extraction without burning the oil or cooking the herb. Allow the oil to cool completely in the pan before straining. Pour into a decorative bottle.

You can use any oil—olive, peanut, corn, canola, you name it—and you should experiment with the herbs as well. Let your imagination run wild. In other words, try any herbs or combination of herbs—basil, thyme, sage, mint. Adjust to your own taste. There is just one important thing you need to remember: a recipe is only a guide; have fun with it.

Flavored oil, in a pretty bottle, with your favorite recipe for using the oil, makes a great gift for the special cooks in your life!

Three Quick and Easy Fresh Herb Condiments

Raspberry and Herb Vinegar

To vinegar, add fresh mint and raspberries. Place bottle in sunny spot for 2 to 3 weeks (shake every other day if you can) before using.

Any fresh herb is great with vinegar: sage, thyme, basil. The French favorite is tarragon; however, I prefer mint and will serve it over fruit salad.

12 oz. white wine vinegar
1 to 2 oz. fresh mint
1 oz. raspberries

Herb Butter (or margarine)

Blend fresh herbs into the butter. Basil, dill, tarragon, or chive butters are great over cooked eggs.

To make garlic butter: to a stick of butter, add 1 tablespoon minced garlic and 3 tablespoons parsley. Place in mold and chill.

1 stick butter or margarine, creamed until fluffy
1/4 cup finely chopped fresh herbs

Herb Jelly

Empty jar of apple jelly into a saucepan. Heat until it is a semi-liquid, then add herbs. Chicken roasted with sage and glazed with sage herb jelly is fabulous. Mint herb jelly is great on lamb or pork. Try tarragon jelly over fish.

10-oz. jar of apple jelly
1/4 cup herbs, finely chopped

Anise

Like its relative fennel, anise has a licorice flavor. It cooks well with root vegetables and adds a nice touch when seasoning chicken or fish. Be careful not to overseason, for a little goes a long way. That is a good rule to remember when using all herbs, fresh or dry.

Basil

This fresh-smelling, sweet-flavored herb is a staple in most Italian kitchens, and it's also believed to be a money charm. The Italian guys I worked with at Balducci's in New York—Gino, Sal, and Mario—all told me that if you keep a fresh basil leaf in your wallet you'll always have money. Every morning those guys would take out the old leaf and replace it with a fresh one. Never worked for me.

Basil is available year-round. During cold months, it's grown in hothouses and sold in small bunches. The quality is excellent, but it can be quite expensive. During the warm seasons, field basil is available; this is the time to make loads of pesto and freeze it for winter. Field basil is about ten times larger than the hothouse type and less than half the price.

This herb is one of the most perishable items in the produce section; therefore, it should be used as soon as possible. If you have to store it, wrap the basil in a wet paper towel, then place it in a plastic bag and refrigerate. It may keep two or three days.

In addition to common basil, over the past few years **red basil** (in the big cities it's called "opal basil") has made an impression on the gourmet scene. It should be selected and stored in the same manner as green basil. Try these two fresh basil recipes:

BAKED TOMATOES

Multiply all ingredients by the number being served.
  For each serving:
    Cut around the stem end of each tomato and remove a cone-shaped plug. Set aside (save!) the plug. Chop the basil and garlic and sprinkle on the cut surface of the tomato. Add a bit of margarine and salt and pepper to taste. Replace the plug and bake in 375 degree oven for about 30 minutes. Discard the plug and serve the tomato on a bed of rice.

tomato, unpeeled
2 to 3 basil leaves
1/2 clove garlic
margarine
salt and pepper

PESTO: THE ITALIAN CLASSIC

Mix ingredients well, add olive oil, and serve. You can also add pignoli or walnuts. Serve over your favorite pasta, vegetables, or shredded cabbage. Great for pizza!

1 cup finely chopped
  basil
2 cloves garlic,
  chopped fine
1/2 oz. chopped
  parsley
1/4 cup olive oil
1/4 cup parmesan
  cheese, grated

Benne (Sesame Seeds)

Sesame Indicum (the plant) is an annual herb grown mostly for its oil-rich seeds. It is among the most ancient of cultivated plants. African slaves introduced benne, as they called the sesame seed, to the southeastern United States. The cooks on the old plantations planted benne to add an African touch to cookies, breads, and cakes.

The seeds are black or white. Half of the seed's weight is from the oil. In America, the oil is used mostly for cooking; in other countries, such as India, the oil is used for lighting and lubrication.

Sesame seeds are loaded with protein, which makes them a great food source for people—and livestock, too.

Some types of sesame plants produce seed pockets that spring open when ripe. That explains the origin of the phrase in the tales of the Arabian Nights—you know, the password "Open sesame!"

BENNE WAFERS

1/2 cup Benne
   (Sesame Seeds)
3/4 cup margarine,
   softened
1 large egg
1-1/2 cups sifted flour
1/2 tsp. baking powder
1 tsp. vanilla extract
1 cup light brown sugar

Mix butter and sugar thoroughly. Add egg. Stir in dry ingredients and vanilla. Drop by teaspoons onto a cookie sheet (leaving extra room to spread). Bake at 325 degrees for about 10 minutes.

Chives

Remember that *herba* means "grass" in Latin? Well, the person who wrote that definition must have been eating chives at the time because they have green, grass-like hollow leaves, and when they're young, they look just like grass.

Although I'm covering chives in the herb section and although most people in the produce business think of them as herbs, they're not. Actually, these Eurasian natives are unusual members of the onion family. They differ from onions in two ways: first, they are so tiny, and, second, their only edible part is the green, grassy top. They have a mild onion flavor and mix very well with the other food groups. Chives and cream cheese makes a delightful spread, and chives and cottage cheese also tastes great. Chives are delicious added to baked potatoes, and the next time you roast a chicken, season it as you usually do, but add about one ounce of finely chopped chives.

Chives come in small bunches and are available year-round. When shopping for them, avoid yellow or slimy leaves. When you get them home, I recommend using them as soon as possible, for the longer they sit, the more flavor is lost. If you have to store chives, place them in a paper bag, then put the bag in a dry place in your refrigerator.

Sometimes you can find planted pots of chives in your produce market. I'm no farmer, but even I can take care of potted chives. You just water them and put them back in the windowsill. The great thing is that you can cut off what you need whenever you want fresh chives, and they grow back.

Cilantro

Cilantro is one of about forty members of the parsley family. In fact, it has the strongest flavor and smell of all the parsleys, though you wouldn't think so to look at it. The leaves are flat and somewhat delicate in shape and color. Bring it to your nose, however, and that strong smell grabs you: refreshing and clean, but not overpowering. The taste is the same—very refreshing.

Cilantro is also known as coriander and as Chinese parsley, and this herb is used quite often in Latin, Hispanic, and Oriental dishes. With its reputation spreading, this herb is surely cutting into mainstream American cuisine. Try adding fresh cilantro to salads with a light dressing. Use it to season beans, meats, and vegetables.

Dill

Today this herb is most often thought of in conjunction with pickles. However, over the centuries dill has been used for many purposes, from cooking to medicine, and even as a deterrent against witches. Its exact origin is unclear, but dill was written about by the early Egyptians some five thousand years ago. The name "dill" comes from the Norwegian word *dilla* ("soothe" or "lull"). The ground herb was fed to babies to soothe their stomachs and lull them to sleep. Fresh dill is still one of nature's best laxatives. At one time, it was believed that hanging fresh dill over the doorway would protect the home from witches and other evils. Dill is used commercially for scenting soaps. However, we care more for its culinary value, right?

Dill can add a new zip to any vegetable dish as well as livening up simple salads. When shopping, avoid dill that has started to yellow and choose dill high in color with a strong aroma; lack of smell is a sign of age, but that is okay if you plan to dry it. The next time you make potato salad, add dill, and for an easy sauce that's excellent with salmon and trout, melt butter or margarine over high heat; while still hot, add fresh chopped dill, then pour over fish.

Marjoram

Now this is an interesting plant. Marjoram is a member of the mint family, and on close inspection of the oval, gray-green leaves and minty aroma, you'll notice the resemblance. Another member of the mint family is oregano (see below), which means that marjoram is a great substitute for oregano, and vice versa. The two plants are very similar in appearance and aroma, although marjoram is not quite as pungent, which may explain why it's not called for as often as its cousin in Italian recipes.

Herbalists credit marjoram with being an excellent remedy for stomach disorders. In cooking, this herb is at its seasoning best when combined with thyme. Marjoram is wonderful when added to meats, fish, vegetables, and stuffing for poultry.

Oregano

The name comes from two Greek words—*oros,* meaning "mountain," and *ganos,* meaning "joy." Centuries ago, oregano and wild marjoram filled the hills of the Mediterranean areas with their beautiful purple flowers and became a symbol of happiness. In Greece, if the plants were found growing on or near a gravesite, it was believed to be a sign that the person buried there was very happy.

During medieval times, an extract from oregano was used to relieve pain from toothaches. This herb is not as rich in color as other fresh herbs, which may be why oregano has a much longer shelf life. With its strong flavor and aroma, oregano truly livens up the dishes it is added to. It's great on pizza or with baked tomatoes or any tomato-based dish.

Parsley

This is the most common herb, but most people don't even think of eating parsley. We think of it as that green stuff that has no purpose and is always on your plate in restaurants. Originally, parsley was put on plates as an after-meal breath freshener; try eating it and notice how clean your mouth and breath feel.

There are nearly forty types of parsley, but in the South, usually only one variety is available: the **Neapolitan**, or curly parsley. Up north and out west the shopper fares a little better. They have two varieties: the curly kind and the flat, broad-leafed **Italian** parsley.

This cousin of the carrot originated in the Mediterranean area. Outside of the United States, it's as popular as it is common, not only as a garnish but also in cooked dishes and as a base green for a salad.

PARSLEY SAUCE

Good with meats and vegetables. Simply excellent over potatoes.

Heat oil and margarine together in a sauté pan. Add onions or shallots if desired. Sauté to almost clear. Add parsley and sauté together to marry flavors.

1 cup parsley, chopped
1 Tbl. margarine
1 Tbl. olive oil
onions or shallots to
taste, chopped

Before I give you a salad recipe, I want you to know how nutritious this herb is. If consumed in larger amounts (three to five ounces), parsley supplies more vitamin A than carrots, more vitamin C than oranges, and about one-third the potassium of a banana. It's also high in calcium, phosphorus, and riboflavin—and low in calories. So with that in mind, eat more parsley.

PARSLEY SALAD

At least 24 hours before serving, mix together all ingredients except parsley. Refrigerate. Thirty minutes before serving, add parsley. Mix. Serve on romaine leaf.

5 tomatoes, chopped
1 cup cracked wheat
1 bunch green onions,
chopped
1/3 cup fresh lemon
juice
1/3 cup virgin olive oil
1 Tbl. pepper
1 oz. fresh mint,
chopped
3 cups parsley leaves,
cleaned, stemmed,
and chopped

Once you get parsley home, plunge the fresh herb into cold water (this extends the storage life), drain, and place in a paper bag. Store in the refrigerator. It should keep for five days.

Rosemary

Rosemary is a symbol of remembrance; in ancient Greece, students wore fresh rosemary in their hair because it was believed to sharpen their memory. During marriage ceremonies, Greek women wore the herb to indicate that they would never forget their families, and the dead were laid to rest with rosemary so they would always be remembered.

Rosemary's culinary values are endless. The ancient cooks discovered that using rosemary helped to tame the tastes of wild meats—rabbit and deer—as well as poultry. Today, rosemary is a "must" on herb racks and in fresh herb gardens. It is still primarily used to season meat and fish or poultry, but I want to point out that it seasons fresh vegetables very well. Try adding rosemary next time you steam veggies, and it's also great with boiled potatoes.

Sage

On first sight, you may wonder if it's vegetable or animal because of its fuzzy, silver leaves. In gourmet kitchens, sage is called the perfect poultry seasoning. Its flavor has been described as musty, which is pretty accurate. Try adding fresh ground sage to your next roasted chicken, but don't stop with poultry, for this herb adds something special when seasoning fish or beef or pork. Fresh sage should be stored in a tightly sealed paper bag, then refrigerated. It should keep for three or four days.

Tarragon

You could call this one the French herb, for its slightly licorice flavor is found in many French dishes. Tarragon is, to my eye, the prettiest of the fresh herbs, with its slender green leaves that bring palm leaves to mind. One of the classic uses for fresh tarragon is to soak it in wine vinegar, and then use the mixture in a number of ways (including pickling and making salad dressing).

PICKLED MELONS

In a large bowl, mix wine and vinegar. Add sugar and herbs, mix until sugar is dissolved. Add melons, then chill at least 3 hours before serving.

2 cups assorted melons, cut into 1-inch squares
2 Tbl. sugar
1/4 cup white wine
1/4 cup vinegar
1 tsp. each fresh dill, tarragon, and mint, finely chopped

Thyme

This is another favorite of the French, though the Creoles of Louisiana are the real thyme-keepers. You can taste thyme in almost every Creole dish, from fish to chicken and from beef to vegetables. Some describe the smell as pungent, and I think its aroma is heavenly—fresh, dried, and while being cooked. The flavor is spicy but not hot. Lemon thyme is also available; it is a wonderful natural blend of thyme with lemon flavor and aroma, excellent with seafoods. Try serving this sauce over your favorite seafood dish: *1 oz. fresh lemon thyme, chopped fine, and 1 oz. fresh dill, chopped, sautéed in margarine, with about 3 oz. cream added and gently heated just before serving.*

NUTS

Nuts are excellent body builders, being great sources of fat, carbohydrates, calcium, protein, and many other nutrients that the body needs for development.

Almonds

There are two kinds of almonds, ***sweet*** and ***bitter.*** The bitter almond is never sold as a table fruit. It is purchased by processors that transform its oil into flavorings and extracts. The sweet almond is the one you will find in your produce section. This one can be subdivided into two groups: soft shell and hard shell. The soft shells are much easier to open, but carry a higher price tag. I think that, though it takes extra time to crack the hard shell, you not only save money with this variety, but also get a much better tasting nut.

California is the world's largest producer of this Mediterranean-basin native. Almonds are available year-round with very few swings in price.

MAMA-IN-LAW ALMOND CRISPS

I gave these cookies their name because they were handed down from Josephine Janisky to her daughter Margaret Janisky Faucett to her daughter Jane Faucett Lehman, then finally to me, her son-in-law at the time. And, now on to you.

1 cup brown sugar
1 cup white sugar
1 lb. butter or
   margarine
3 eggs
2 tsp. vanilla extract
1 tsp. salt
4-1/2 cups flour
2 tsp. baking soda
1 cup sliced almonds

Cream sugars and softened margarine together. Stir in vanilla. Add eggs one at a time, beating each into the mixture. Sift flour, salt, and soda together and add to the egg mixture a little at a time, mixing well. Fold in sliced almonds.

Divide into four equal sections and form into round loaves. Wrap each loaf in wax paper and chill thoroughly or freeze overnight.

Slice thin and bake in 375 degree oven for about 10 minutes or until brown.

Brazil Nuts

I loved these nuts as a kid, but they are so hard to crack! If you saw a Brazil nut fresh from the tree, you might mistake it for a coconut, they look so much alike. That is where the similarities end, though, because beneath the shell, instead of liquid, you will find about twenty tightly fitting segments. These are the Brazil nuts you are used to finding in the produce section. Although Brazil nuts have a very hard shell and hard meat, they will spoil if not stored properly in a cool, dry area.

Cashews

Another South American native nut is the cashew. Nowadays, the majority of the cashews we consume come from India. Believe it or not, this nut is related to one of my favorite tropical fruits—mangoes. With the mango, you eat the meat and throw away the seed. With cashews, however, you discard the flesh or meat, and roast and enjoy the seed. In the supermarket you will find shelled and roasted, sometimes raw, cashews.

Chestnuts

In most of the gourmet shops, you will find chestnuts imported from Italy, but not because that's the best chestnut of all time. Around the turn of the century, three types of chestnuts were available: Oriental, European, and American. The American chestnut is believed to have been the best chestnut of all. Unfortunately, during that same period of time, a chestnut blight totally wiped out the American chestnut tree.

Chestnuts are usually priced according to size (medium, large, and extra large or jumbo). Different areas of the country use different labels to determine size. Normally, the larger the size, the higher the price. I can't determine a big enough difference in taste from large to small to pay the difference in price, so my recommendation is for the less expensive ones. Most of us know of roasting chestnuts, but here is a French dessert topping you may want to try during the holiday season: Take chestnut meat and boil it in sugar syrup with vanilla flavoring. Creamed marrons, as this dish is known, is scrumptious.

Hazelnuts

My appreciation for this nut didn't develop until my first trip to Europe. Being a Southerner, I was much more familiar with pecans, peanuts, and black walnuts. During the holiday season I always skimmed over the smooth, hard-shelled, round brown things that reminded me of large acorns. In Europe, though, the hazelnut (also called "filbert" because the first day of harvest is August 22—St. Filbert's Day) is everywhere. It is used as a table food, is great in baking, and mixes well with chocolate. In fact, I first tasted this nut in a candy bar in Paris. I asked my companion about it, and then went out and bought two kilos to take back to our hotel. Turkey is by far the world's largest producer of the hazelnut; next is Italy, and there is a small crop grown in the western United States.

Macadamia Nuts

These nuts are not native to Hawaii, as many people think. They originated in Australia, then were transplanted to Hawaii, where, along with pineapples, they have become a major export and cash crop. Macadamias are one of the most oily and flavorful nuts of all. Unshelled, this nut looks very similar to the hazelnut, except that the macadamia's shell is as hard as a rock. In fact, it takes some 350 pounds of pressure per square inch to crack one, so please never try it with your teeth. The macadamia is high in price and fat, but it is also a good source of protein, calcium, and carbohydrates.

Peanuts

My home state of Georgia may no longer lead the nation in peach production, but it is still number one in peanuts. The peanut is really a member of the legume family, the same as peas and beans, except for one difference: the peanut is developed underground. It is called "ground nut" in some places. Peanuts are available year-round in one form or another. They are an excellent source of protein.

Pecans

Most years, Georgia produces more than half of all the pecans sold in America. In fact, there is only one other nut more popular than our southern pecan: the walnut. The pecan is native to North America. There are very few, if any, pecan trees in Europe. So if you have friends in Europe and want to impress them with your gourmet gifts, send pecans or pecan candies.

Pistachios

When I was a kid someone asked if I would like to try pistachio ice cream. I said, "No way." I thought it was some weird flavor like licorice, and I didn't want to have any part of it. I think I had my first pistachio nut at age twenty. It was love at first crack.

Iran and Turkey lead the world production of this light green nut, which belongs to the same family as cashews and mangoes. Nowadays, in your produce market, you can find pistachios from California as well. The meat is light green, but the hard shell is almost colorless in its natural tone. Some processors color this nut red before shipping to market. I opt for the natural color if I have a choice. Most pistachios are partially cracked because of that extremely hard shell. The slight crack makes it easier for the consumer to get at the goody.

Walnuts

I grew up eating black walnuts. They're tough to crack, but they sure are great eating.

Unfortunately, to some people the black walnut tree is more valuable as a source of wood for furniture and gunstocks than as a food source, so there are very few black walnut trees around. But if you're ever down in Conyers, Georgia, you can come by my house and take a look at my tree; it's old and beautiful.

The English walnut, which is one of the world's most popular nuts, was brought to America from southern Europe. California and Oregon are both major producers. Unlike its native American cousin, the English walnuts have thin shells that crack easily and yield much more of the mild, sweet meat.

Curtis Aikens'

Recipes

Soups

Salads & Dressings

Sauces & Dips

Fruits & Vegetables

Main Dishes

Desserts

Breadstuffs

SOUPS

CURTIS'S MINESTRONE

8 oz. white cannellini beans
   *(if dry, soak overnight
   in cold water)*
3 Tbl. olive oil
1 turkey leg
1 onion, chopped
2 cloves garlic, minced
4 sticks celery, chopped
2 carrots, diced
1 small head savoy or green
   cabbage, shredded
4 oz. green beans cut into
   1-inch pieces
8 oz. tomatoes, diced
1 dried red chile
10 cups water
1 sprig fresh rosemary
1 bay leaf
12 oz. pasta
3 zucchini, peeled and diced
1 Tbl. each fresh chopped
   basil and parsley
salt and pepper

In a large pot add oil, turkey leg, onion and garlic; sauté until onions are soft. Add celery, carrots, cabbage, and green beans. Drain and add beans to pot along with tomatoes and chile. Add water and bring to boil. Add rosemary and bay leaf. Simmer uncovered about 1-1/2 hours. Add pasta; cook about 10 minutes. Add zucchini. Cook about 20 minutes more. Remove rosemary and bay leaf. Add basil and parsley. Salt and pepper to taste.

POTATO LEEK SOUP

3 oz. margarine
4 leeks, chopped
2 stalks celery, peeled and
   diced
1 onion, chopped
3 large potatoes, chopped
1-1/2 qts. water
1-1/2 cups cream
salt and pepper to taste

In a large pot, add margarine, leeks, celery, and onion. Sauté about 8 minutes. Add potatoes and water and bring to boil. Lower heat and simmer about 30 minutes. During the last 5 minutes of cooking, add cream and seasoning. *(Don't forget the garlic bread!)*

CREAM OF BROCCOLI, CAULIFLOWER, OR CELERY SOUP

(Just exchange the vegetables)

Place 1 cup broccoli and 1 cup carrots in a pan. Add 1 cup broth. Cook until tender, about 4 minutes. Drain and set aside. In a large pot, add margarine. Sauté onions until clear; add flour and cook about 2 minutes. DO NOT BROWN. Add chicken broth. Whisk well until mixture boils, being sure to reach bottom of pan. Simmer about 30 minutes. Strain off vegetables and place into a blender with 1-1/2 cups liquid; purée. Stir back into pot with remaining broth. Stir in cream and set aside cooked vegetables. Heat and serve.

2 cups chopped broccoli (or cauliflower or celery)
2 carrots, diced
4 Tbl. margarine
2 cups onions, diced
3 Tbl. flour
6 cups hot chicken broth
salt and pepper to taste
1 cup whipping cream

GEORGIA'S ONION SOUP

(Use Vidalia onions when available)

In a pot, sauté onions with margarine until soft. Add broth, wine, seasoning, and herbs. I use tarragon and sage. Simmer about 35 minutes. In a serving bowl, place a slice of cornbread. Sprinkle with cheese. Add soup and serve.

4 onions, sliced
4 Tbl. margarine
4 cups chicken broth
1 cup white wine
salt and pepper to taste
2 Tbl. fresh chopped herbs
(your favorites)
cornbread or muffins
cheese *(I like cheddar; try your favorite)*

Jack-O'-Lantern Soup

1 pumpkin top, carved and
 inside cleaned
1/2 lb. sugar pumpkin,
 cubed
4 Tbl. melted margarine
salt and pepper
1 cup onion, chopped
1/2 cup each chopped
 carrots and celery
4 cups chicken broth
1 cup tomatoes, diced
1/4 cup rice

Coat inside of pumpkin with half the melted margarine and sprinkle inside with salt and pepper. Bake in 400 degree oven 20 minutes. Sauté mixed vetetables in remaining margarine about 5 minutes. Add broth. Bring to boil. Pour broth and vegetables along with rice into pumpkin. Return to oven with lid on top. Bake about 60 minutes or until pumpkin is tender, but not too soft. Place whole pumpkin on dinner table.

Chicken Soup

One of the dishes I made for Evander Holyfield out in Reno. (Of course you don't have to make this much; I was feeding 7 or 8 huge guys.)

8 lbs. chicken, cut into bite-
 sized pieces
2 large onions, chopped
2 leeks, chopped
1 bunch celery, chopped
1 bunch broccoli, chopped
2 lbs. carrots, chopped
margarine
Worcestershire sauce
salt and pepper
a bit of sage
water

In a pot, sauté chicken in margarine and Worcestershire sauce about 4 minutes. Add 2 or 3 cups of water and chicken bones. Boil 20 to 30 minutes to ensure a thick broth. Remove bones. Reduce heat and add onion and leeks. Sauté all other chopped vegetables together in margarine for about 3 minutes. Salt and pepper to taste, then transfer sautéed vegetables into chicken broth. Simmer about 40 minutes. Serve with cornbread.

GROUND TURKEY SOUP

In a large pot, sauté turkey with margarine and herbs for about 6 minutes. Add vegetables and cook 5 minutes more. Add water and simmer about 1-1/2 hours.

1 lb. ground turkey
5 cups water
4 onions, chopped
4 carrots, chopped
4 celery ribs, chopped
6 tomatoes, diced
4 potatoes, peeled and diced
1/2 broccoli head, chopped
salt and pepper to taste
1 oz. each fresh thyme and
    sage, chopped
2 Tbl. margarine

VEGETARIAN CHILI

In a large pot, add margarine, onions, and garlic. Sauté until onions are clear. Add mushrooms and pepper. Cook about 2 minutes. Add tomatoes, beans, and chili powder. Simmer about 45 minutes. Season to taste.

2 Tbl. margarine
1 onion, chopped
2 cloves garlic, chopped
1 cup mushrooms, sliced
1 green pepper, chopped
4 cups red kidney beans,
    canned or cooked
8 tomatoes, chopped
2 Tbl. chili powder *(if you
    like it hot, add chopped
    jalapeño pepper)*

MY FAVORITE QUICK BROTH

Juice fresh celery and onion together. Heat in a small saucepan until almost clear. Season to taste with herbs, salt, and pepper. When I'm using this broth as a starter for potato soup, I use thyme and sage; for tomato soup, basil and oregano.

VEGETABLE BROTH

1 small onion, chopped
1 stalk celery, chopped
1 bay leaf
1 oz. parsley, chopped
4 cups of water

In a large saucepan, sauté onion and celery in oil about 10 minutes; add bay leaf and parsley. Sauté 5 minutes longer and add water. Bring up to rapid boil, lower heat and simmer one hour. Season with salt and pepper. Remove vegetables and there you have your clear broth. Depending on how you are using the broth, you may want to purée the veggies and add them to the pot.

CARROT WITH ORANGE SOUP

This is my version of a wonderful soup served in a Marin County restaurant.

10 carrots, cleaned and sliced
1-1/2 to 2 cups water
half an onion, diced
1 or 2 cloves of garlic,
    minced
2 Tbl. butter or margarine
1 small sweet orange (or a
    quarter of a large)

To a soup pot add carrots, enough water to just cover the carrots, 1 tablespoon margarine, and a bit of salt and pepper. Boil until carrots are tender (10 to 25 minutes depending on the thickness of your slices).

While carrots are cooking, dice orange and set aside. Sauté onion and garlic with remaining margarine until onion is clear (about 4 minutes). Remove carrots from pot and place along with sautéed vegetables and orange in a blender. Purée. Return puréed vegetables to carrot broth and simmer until ready to serve.

This soup is great served in a hollowed out multigrain loaf or roll.

SALADS & DRESSINGS

French Salad and Dressing

Salad

1 head romaine lettuce,
    washed and cut into
    bite-sized pieces
2 hard-boiled eggs, quartered
6 anchovies, chopped
    (optional)
10 pitted black olives
1/4 cucumber, diced
1 can tuna, drained
4 large artichoke hearts,
    quartered

Set eggs aside. In a large salad bowl add romaine and all remaining salad ingredients and toss. Add eggs.

Dressing

1/3 cup olive oil
2 Tbl. white wine
1/2 clove garlic, chopped
1 tsp. mustard
juice of 1/2 lemon

Mix dressing ingredients. Pour over salad, toss again, and serve. Salt to taste.

Butter Bean and Tuna Salad

1 lb. cooked butter beans *(if
    you can't find fresh, you
    may use frozen)*
6 oz. canned tuna
juice of one lemon
1 oz. blend of fresh chopped
    herbs of your choice *(I
    use tarragon and sage)*
8 Tbl. olive oil
salt and pepper to taste
6 plum tomatoes, sliced

In a shallow serving dish, place beans. Add tuna to beans. Mix together lemon juice, herbs, and olive oil. Add to beans. Toss and season with salt and pepper. Surround salad with sliced plum tomatoes and serve.

QUILLA'S CARROT SALAD

Combine all ingredients; toss and serve. Quilla tells me to make the salad a day ahead in order to get the best flavor.

4 lbs. carrots, grated
3 Tbl. sugar
1 lb. raisins
2 cups pineapple, diced
3 Tbl. mayonnaise

DANDELION SALAD WITH ORANGE SOY DRESSING

Choose a pound of dandelion leaves; the smaller and younger the better. Wash and dry carefully. Set aside. In a mixing bowl, add orange juice, orange peel, soy sauce, ginger, olive oil, and garlic. Add salt and pepper to taste. When ready to serve, pour over dandelion greens. Toss.

1 lb. dandelion leaves
1/2 cup fresh orange juice
1 tsp. grated orange peel
2 Tbl. soy sauce
1 tsp. grated fresh ginger
3 Tbl. olive oil
1 clove garlic, chopped fine
salt and pepper to taste

Beets and Pears with Dandelion Greens and Mustard Vinaigrette

Vinaigrette

2 Tbl. Dijon mustard
2 Tbl. mild red onions, finely chopped
2 Tbl. distilled white vinegar
1/3 cup salad oil

Mix all ingredients together.

Other Ingredients

1 medium pear
3 cups young, tender dandelion greens
2 medium beets, cooked, peeled, and cut into 1/8-inch strips
1 to 2 Tbl. finely chopped nuts (*your favorite*)

Peel and core pear, cut into 1/8-inch strips, and immediately mix with vinaigrette to prevent darkening. Arrange dandelion greens evenly on 4 serving plates. Make 2 or 3 alternating layers of beets and pears on each plate. Pour vinaigrette dressing over your salad. Sprinkle nuts on top and serve.

Yam Salad

3 large yams, boiled, peeled, and sliced
1 large sweet onion, sliced thin
one-half each green, yellow, and red pepper, sliced into strips
4 oz. vinaigrette dressing and 2 oz. honey, mixed

Mix all ingredients in a large bowl. Chill (overnight for best flavor) before serving.

MAMA'S POTATO SALAD

Combine all ingredients. Mix well. Chill and serve.

4 potatoes, boiled, peeled,
  and diced *(cool)*
3 hard-boiled eggs, chopped
  (cool)
1 celery rib, diced
one-quarter pepper, diced
1 small onion, diced
2 Tbl. pimiento
2 Tbl. sweet relish
4 Tbl. mayonnaise
1 Tbl. mustard
1/2 tsp. each salt, pepper,
  and sugar

MAMA'S COLE SLAW

Mix all ingredients. Chill thoroughly and serve.

1 medium cabbage, grated
1 onion, grated
1 carrot, grated
1 pepper, chopped
2 Tbl. sweet relish
1/2 cup mayonnaise
1 Tbl. sugar
1/2 tsp. lemon juice
1/2 tsp. vinegar

SALAD NEW ORLEANS

Toss all ingredients; let stand about 1 hour to blend flavors. Chill and serve.

5 tomatoes, diced
8 zucchini, sliced
1 each red, yellow, and green
  pepper, chopped
1 avocado, diced
1 onion, chopped
3 green onions, chopped
2 tsp. sugar
salt and pepper to taste

MY SPRING HARVEST SALAD WITH PASTA

8 to 12 oz. pasta, cooked and
    cooled
4 oz. snow peas
2 big broccoli tops
1-1/2 cups fresh pineapple,
    cubed
1 large Vidalia onion, diced
2 ribs celery, diced
salad dressing

Steam snow peas and broccoli florets for about 4 minutes. Mix all ingredients together and add your favorite dressing. I like a vinaigrette. Chill and serve.

ALL-AMERICAN SALAD

1 small head red cabbage,
    grated
1 large carrot, grated
1 medium Wisconsin Red
    apple, cored and
    chopped
juice from (at least) half a Key
    lime
25 white seedless grapes,
    sliced
1/2 cup walnuts, chopped
3/4 cup raisins *(golden
    raisins look best but I
    prefer regular for taste)*
1/2 sweet white onion,
    chopped
4 Tbl. mayonnaise

In the order listed, add ingredients in a large bowl. Stir well after adding the lime juice, and at the end.

30 MINUTE GOURMET MEAL

TERESA'S SALAD WITH POPPY SEED DRESSING

Mix all ingredients. Pour over a bowl of fresh greens in any combination you like. You can include tomatoes, cucumbers, onion, radishes, etc. Toss. Serve with garlic bread!

1 cup vinegar
2 Tbl. poppy seeds
1 to 2 Tbl. sugar *(or juice concentrate)*
1 hard-boiled egg, finely chopped

GARLIC BREAD

Slice Italian or French-type bread lengthwise. Spread with butter. Sprinkle with garlic salt. Broil until brown. Slice into 2-inch pieces. Serve hot.

THREE BEAN SALAD

(This is one of the few salads in which I will use canned vegetables.)

Mix all ingredients in a large bowl. Chill a day ahead.

1 15-oz. can each of red kidney, green, and garbonzo beans, drained
1/2 cup sugar
1/2 cup olive oil
one-half each red, yellow, and green pepper, chopped
1 onion, sliced into rings
1 oz. each tarragon and basil, chopped
2 oz. parsley, chopped
1/2 tsp. dry mustard
1/2 cup vinegar

HARVEST SALAD WITH MARMALADE DRESSING

2 ribs of celery, chopped
2 broccoli tops, cut *(not chopped)*
1/2 head of cauliflower, cut into 1-inch pieces
1/2 bunch green onions, chopped
3 carrots, diced
some of your favorite spring vegetables
Marmalade Dressing *(below)*

Prepare dressing and allow to cool. Parboil all vegetables except the onion for 4 minutes. Combine with onion in a large bowl. Toss with dressing and serve.

MARMALADE DRESSING

1/2 cup Orange Marmalade
1/2 fresh pineapple, chopped
1/2 cup sugar
1/2 cup water
1/2 cup vinegar
1 Tbl. soy sauce

In a sauce pan, add pineapple, sugar, water, and vinegar. Bring to boil, stirring. Add marmalade.

If the dressing is too thin, mix 2 tablespoons cornstarch with 2 tablespoons cold water until smooth. Add to hot mixture and stir until thick. Allow to cool. Toss with salad and serve.

JENNY'S HERBAL SALAD DRESSING

1 cup oil
1/2 cup white wine vinegar
1 Tbl. Dijon mustard
2 tsp. horseradish
2 tsp. sugar
1 oz. fresh tarragon, chopped
2-1/2 oz. fresh basil, chopped
half an onion, chopped
1 Tbl. lemon juice
2 Tbl. Lawry's seasoning
3/4 tsp. black pepper
2 cloves garlic, chopped

Mix all ingredients together. Serve over your favorite salad. For best flavor, make 24 hours ahead.

CAESAR SALAD DRESSING

Mix all ingredients well. Serve over Romaine lettuce and croutons.

2 cloves garlic, chopped
6 Tbl. olive oil
4 Tbl. lemon juice
2 Tbl. Worcestershire sauce
1/2 tsp. pepper
1 hard or soft-boiled egg, mashed
5 Tbl. grated Parmesan cheese
8 anchovies, chopped fine

EGGPLANT SALAD DRESSING

Cut eggplant into 1-inch pieces; salt, place in colander. Cover with a plate and put something heavy on top. Anything heavy will do. A bowl of fruit is perfect. Allow the bitter juices to drain about 20 minutes. Pat dry and place in a baking pan. Cover with garlic and oil. Bake at 400 degrees about 15 minutes, or until tender and brown. Cool and pour into a mixing bowl. Add remaining ingredients. Mix well. Great on salad or potato dishes.

2 eggplants
3 cloves garlic, chopped
1/2 cup oil
1/3 cup vinegar
1/3 cup white wine
salt and pepper

ALL APPLE SALAD WITH FLORIDA DRESSING

Place apples in a large bowl. Stir juices into yogurt a little at a time to desired consistency. Spoon or pour over apples. Chill and serve.

6 apples of different varieties, cored and diced
1 4-oz. container strawberry yogurt
juice from 4 different Florida citruses (1 Valencia, 1 navel, 1 tangerine, 1 tangelo)

2 ripe bananas, mashed
1 tsp. dry mustard
1 cup sour cream
1/2 cup sugar
1 tsp. salt
2 Tbl. orange juice

BANANA SALAD DRESSING

Blend all ingredients together. Chill before using. For salad or fruits.

1/2 cup pineapple, chopped
4 Tbl. white wine
2 Tbl. vinegar
2 cloves garlic, chopped
1 oz. each fresh basil and
    marjoram, chopped

FRESH PINEAPPLE DRESSING

Mix all ingredients. Serve over salad greens or baked potato.

SAUCES & DIPS

GINGER GARLIC DIP

2 oz. fresh ginger, finely
    chopped
3 cloves garlic, finely chopped
1 cup mayonnaise
1 cup sour cream
1/4 cup chopped parsley
1/4 cup water chestnuts (or
    peeled Jicama), finely
    chopped
1-1/2 Tbl. soy sauce

Mix all ingredients well. Chill and serve with vegetables.

MUSTARD SAUCE

5 Tbl. dry mustard
1/4 cup melted margarine
1 egg, beaten
4 Tbl. white wine
1/2 cup milk

Mix ingredients, simmer about 10 minutes. Be careful not to burn. Great on stir-fried oriental vegetables.

CAJUN MARINADE

(a Cajun start for your favorite recipes)

1 Tbl. lime juice
1/2 tsp. garlic powder
1/2 tsp. onion powder
1/4 tsp. thyme leaves, crushed
1/4 tsp. salt
1/8 to 1/4 tsp. ground red
    pepper
1/8 tsp. ground black pepper

Mix all ingredients. Marinate shrimp, chicken, or vegetables. Cook as usual.

DANDELION SPREAD

Combine in a blender dandelion greens, cottage cheese, and chopped nuts. Add dressing a little at a time to make mixture the right consistency to spread onto crackers. Makes 1/4 to 3/4 cups of spread.

1 cup young, tender
  dandelion greens
1/2 cup cottage cheese
1 qt. chopped nuts *(pecans, walnuts, or whatever you desire)*
your favorite salad dressing

PESTO WITH PECANS

In a food processor, blend basil, garlic, and nuts. Place in a mixing bowl. Add cheese and oil. Mix well. Serve over noodles.

2 cups fresh basil
5 cloves garlic
1/3 cup pecans
3/4 cup grated Parmesan
  cheese
3/4 cup olive oil

SALSA

Mix all ingredients. Chill about 30 minutes before serving.

4 large, ripe tomatoes,
  chopped
1 large onion, chopped
5 or 6 chili peppers, chopped
1/2 cup taco sauce
1 oz. fresh cilantro, chopped

EASY DIP

2 vegetables *(broccoli and*
    cauliflower or any of
    your favorites)
1/2 cup sour cream or
    mayonnaise
1 shallot, chopped
1/4 tsp. dry mustard
1/4 tsp. each dried thyme
    and tarragon

Steam vegetables until tender, then purée. Mix in remaining ingredients. Great with chips or raw vegetables.

SIMPLE PASTA SAUCE

1/4 stick margarine
1 medium onion, chopped
1/2 cup whipping cream
1/2 Tbl. basil
1/2 cup chicken broth

In a saucepan, melt margarine and add onion. Sauté. Add whipping cream, basil, and chicken broth. Cook until thick. Pour over noodles.

PEANUT SAUCE

1/4 cup creamy peanut
    butter
1/4 cup plum jam
1 Tbl. lemon juice
1 Tbl. soy sauce
Tabasco sauce

In a mixing bowl, combine first four ingredients. Season with Tabasco. Wonderful as vegetable dip or with fruits.

PINEAPPLE AND PECAN SPREAD

1 cup fresh pineapple, diced
1 cup sugar
1/2 cup pecans, chopped
3 Tbl. mayonnaise

In a saucepan, add pineapple with its juice, and sugar. Cook until thick. Add nuts. Mix and let cool before serving. Try this on pound cake or toasted raisin bread. It's terrific!

VEGETARIAN GRAVY

In a large pan, sauté onion in oil until very brown. Push onion to the sides. In the center, add margarine and allow to melt before adding flour. Stir together to blend well and continue stirring until margarine and flour are bubbling happily. Stir and cook the roux about two minutes. Remove roux from heat and wait for bubbling to stop. All at once add broth and return to heat. Whisk over medium heat until gravy thickens. When thick, add sherry and season to taste. You can remove the onion with a strainer if you like, but I think it adds character. Great over hot biscuits.

1 medium onion, chopped fine
3 Tbl. oil
3 Tbl. margarine
3 Tbl. flour
2 cups Vegetable Broth *(recipe on page 160)*
2 Tbl. dry sherry
salt and pepper to taste

NATURAL SWEET AND SOUR SAUCE

Try this with my Country Tempura, page 178.

In a sauce pan, melt margarine. Add garlic and onions, simmer about 3 minutes. Raise heat and add peppers; sauté about 3 minutes longer. Add fruit and sauté at least 4 minutes. Add juice and soy sauce when ready to serve.

2 Tbl. margarine
2 cloves of garlic, finely chopped
half an onion, chopped
one-half each red and green pepper, sliced into thin strips
1 peach, sliced
1 nectarine, sliced
1 plum, sliced
1 cup grapes, sliced
1/4 cup fresh orange juice
1/4 cup soy sauce

FRUITS & VEGETABLES

COUNTRY TEMPURA

vegetables, only your favorites
2 eggs, beaten
1/4 cup cornmeal
1 cup flour
1/4 tsp. garlic powder
salt and pepper, about
    1/4 tsp. each

Mix dry ingredients together. Cut your favorite vegetables into bite-size pieces. Dip veggies in egg, then roll in flour mixture and deep fry. Serve with blue cheese or horseradish dip. This is also great with my Natural Sweet and Sour Sauce *(recipe on page 175)*.

ZUCCHINI IN WHITE WINE SAUCE

2 cups zucchini, sliced
1/2 cup onion, sliced
2 Tbl. margarine
2 Tbl. flour
4 oz. cream
1/4 cup Chardonnay
2 Tbl. parsley, chopped
1/4 tsp. Worcestershire
    sauce
salt and pepper to taste

Steam zucchini and onion about 4 minutes. In a saucepan, melt margarine. Add flour and cream, constantly stirring until smooth. Add half the parsley, and all the Worcestershire sauce and seasoning. Add Chardonnay. Stir slowly and constantly. Remove from heat. Place vegetables in a casserole dish. Cover with wine sauce. Add remaining parsley. Bake in 350 degree oven until bubbly. Add cheese if you care to.

THE WAY MAMA FRIES CORN FOR THREE

5 to 6 ears corn (cut kernels
    from the cob;
    see page 83)
1/4 cup oil
1 cup water
2 Tbl. flour
salt and pepper to taste

In a large frying pan, heat oil (very hot). Mix corn, flour, and seasoning; add water. Add to frying pan. Add more water if needed. Fry about 7 minutes. Lower heat, let simmer about 30 more minutes.

OUT OF THIS WORLD BASIC BEANS

Soak dried beans overnight. Rinse and re-cover beans with water. Using enough oil to cover the bottom of a large pot, warm onion, garlic, celery, and herbs. Add water and beans. Simmer about 3 hours, adding water as necessary to just cover beans. When beans are tender, remove about a cup of cooked beans and mash into paste. Return paste to bean pot and stir until thickened. Serve alone or over rice. Garnish as desired and serve with Tabasco.

2 lbs. dried beans (red kidney, black, or navy)
1 pot water
2 large onions, chopped
4 cloves garlic, chopped
1/2 cup celery, chopped
2 tsp. salt
1/4 tsp. thyme
2 bay leaves
oil
Tabasco sauce, optional

LIMA BEANS AND HERBS

In a saucepan, combine turkey and cream. Add salt and pepper. Bring to boil until cream thickens, about 6 minutes. Place limas in a serving dish and keep warm. Add cream with turkey and chopped herbs, then toss and serve.

2 lbs. cooked lima beans *(if fresh are not available, use frozen)*
1/2 cup heavy cream
3 oz. cooked turkey breast, sliced into thin strips
2 Tbl. fresh parsley, chopped
2 Tbl. fresh chervil, chopped

RED BEANS AND RICE

1 lb. dried red kidney beans
1 pot water
2 chicken backs or legs
1 large onion, chopped
2 cloves garlic, chopped
1/4 cup celery, chopped
1/2 tsp. Tabasco
    sauce *(optional)*
1 tsp. salt
1/4 tsp. thyme
1 bay leaf
3 cups hot cooked rice

Soak beans in water overnight. Pour into a large pot. Add remaining ingredients, except rice. Simmer about 3 hours, or until beans are tender. Add water when necessary during cooking. Water should just cover beans when cooking ends. Remove 1 cup of cooked beans and mash into paste. Pour back into pot. Stir until liquid is thickened. Serve over rice.

POTATOES GOLD

1 clove garlic, chopped
2 Tbl. margarine
2-1/2 lbs. potatoes, peeled
    and sliced very thin
1/2 cup cream
1-1/2 cups grated
    Gruyère cheese
1/3 cup margarine,
    cut into small pieces
salt and pepper to taste

Use a heavy baking dish which can double as a serving dish. Rub bottom and sides with garlic and margarine. Place half the potatoes in bottom; cover with half the cheese and seasoning. Dot with margarine. Cover that with remaining potatoes, then the last of the cheese. Pour cream into side of dish around potatoes. Bake in preheated 400 degree oven until potatoes are golden brown, about 40 minutes.

HARICOTS VERTS *(FRENCH BEANS)*

Cut tops and tails off beans, then cook them in boiling water about 12 minutes. While beans are cooking, fry chopped onions in the margarine until onions are golden brown—not burned. Drain beans and toss to dry. Pour onion and margarine over beans and serve. Season with salt and pepper.

1 lb. French beans
  (if not available, use very small green beans)
1 oz. margarine
1 medium onion, chopped
salt and pepper to taste

RED PEARS

In a medium pot, add wine, lemon juice, peel, sugar, and cinnamon. Bring to boil, stir to dissolve sugar. Remove eyes from bottom of pears, then add to wine. Lower heat and simmer about 20 minutes. Be sure wine covers all of the pears. Allow pears to cool in the syrup. Remove cinnamon stick and lemon peel and discard. Place pears in a serving dish. Spoon syrup over pears. Serve warm or chilled.

2 cups dry red wine
juice of 1/2 lemon
1 strip lemon peel
1 small piece of cinnamon
6 small Comice pears peeled,
  with stems left on

ZUCCHINI CASSEROLE

Steam zucchini and cool. In a casserole dish add zucchini, crumbled bread, milk, and eggs. Bake in 375 degree oven 25 to 30 minutes.

2 zucchinis, sliced
1 onion, sliced
4 slices bread, broken up
2 cups milk
4 large eggs, beaten
salt and pepper to taste

Curtis Aikens' Stuffed Zucchini

1 large zucchini
1/4 lb. ground turkey
1 small onion, chopped
2 cloves garlic, chopped
half a bell pepper, chopped
1/2 lb. grated cheese
2 Tbl. Worcestershire sauce
salt and pepper to taste

Slice zucchini about 3/4 inch from blossom end. Take the large portion and core it. Set aside. Combine remaining ingredients. Mix well. Stuff zucchini with turkey mixture. Bake at 425 degrees for about 35 minutes. Slice into rings. Sprinkle with cheese.

Stuffed Chayote Squash

2 Chayote squashes
4 oz. ground turkey
2 oz. each red, green, and
    yellow pepper, chopped
3 oz. onion, chopped
1 oz. olive oil
4 oz. grated cheese

Slice chayotes in half. Boil in salty water for about 30 minutes. Scoop out seeds and discard. Scoop out flesh and mix with all other ingredients except cheese. Sauté with olive oil. Stuff sautéed vegetables in squash halves, then bake in 325 degree oven about 20 minutes. Sprinkle with cheese and serve.

Stuffed Peppers

1-1/2 cups cooked rice
1/2 lb. ground turkey
1 onion, chopped
1 tsp. salt
1 carrot, diced
1/2 cup celery, chopped
5 or 6 cored peppers

Sauté turkey and chopped vegetables. Season and add rice. Stuff into pepper and bake at 350 degrees for about 30 minutes. Add cheese topping if you like.

GLAZED ONIONS

Place onions in a baking dish. Add seasoning and butter. Pour honey over onions. Bake in 450 degree oven for about 1 hour.

15 small onions, peeled
10 tsp. honey
4 Tbl. butter or margarine
1/2 tsp. salt
1/4 tsp. pepper

ASPARAGUS AND PARMESAN

Place asparagus in a shallow pan and pour other ingredients over it. Place under broiler for about 3 minutes. Serve. *You may use other vegetables as well.*

1/2 lb. steamed asparagus
3 Tbl. melted margarine
2 Tbl. lemon juice
4 Tbl. grated Parmesan cheese

MAMA'S COLLARDS

Boil chicken about 20 minutes. Add collards and seasoning. Lower heat, cook about 2 hours or until greens are tender.

1 bunch collards, stemmed, washed very well,and torn into small pieces
2-1/4 cups water
2 chicken thighs
light salt and pepper to taste

MAMA'S FRIED OKRA

(You will love it.)

Wash and cut okra into 1/4-inch pieces. Mix corn meal, flour, and seasoning. Add okra. Pour oil into a deep frying pan and heat to about 400 degrees. Fry okra and corn meal mixture.

2 lbs. okra
1/2 cup self-rising corn meal
2 Tbl. self-rising flour
1-1/2 cups oil
dash salt and pepper

MAMA'S GREEN BEANS

green beans cut into
    1/2-inch pieces
2 cups water
1 Tbl. salt
1/4 cup oil

In a medium pot, boil water. Add salt, oil, and beans. Lower heat and simmer about 1-1/2 hours. During the last 30 minutes, add peeled and quartered potatoes and pepper if you like.

MAMA'S CANDIED SWEET POTATOES

4 sweet potatoes, cooked,
    peeled, and sliced
1/2 cup water
1-1/2 cups sugar
1 stick margarine
1 tsp. lemon juice
1 Tbl. vanilla

In a boiler, add water, sweet potatoes, and sugar. Boil. Add margarine, juice, and vanilla. Lower heat after 15 minutes. Simmer 20 minutes longer.

MARINATED MUSHROOMS

(other veggies can be substituted)

2 lbs. button mushrooms,
    washed and trimmed
1 cup olive oil
1/2 cup white wine vinegar
4 Tbl. lemon juice
2 bunches green onions,
    chopped
1/2 cup parsley, chopped
1 oz. fresh tarragon, chopped
2 tsp. salt
2 tsp. sugar

While mushrooms dry, mix all other ingredients and pour over mushrooms. Cover and refrigerate at least 1 day ahead.

MARINATED ARTICHOKES
Use 2 lbs. baby artichokes in place of mushrooms above. Steam 'chokes until leaves are loose and tender.

STUFFED MUSHROOMS

Brush mushrooms with half the olive oil; set aside. In a frying pan, sauté next 3 ingredients with remaining olive oil. Spoon on top of each mushroom. Fry bread crumbs in margarine; place on top of stuffing. Sprinkle with Parmesan cheese. Bake at 425 degrees for about 7 or 8 minutes.

15 jumbo mushrooms, washed, stems cut off
4 Tbl. olive oil
1 small onion, chopped
6 oz. ground turkey
1 oz. Super Sauce *(recipe on page 193)*
1 tsp. margarine
2 oz. bread crumbs

EASY SWISS CHARD SIDE DISH

Wash chard and drain. In a saucepan heat water to boiling; add a pinch of salt if desired. Place chard in water and cover pan tightly. Steam for about 4 minutes until tender-crisp. Meanwhile, heat oil in a skillet, add onion, and cook until transparent. Add garlic to the onions and stir until chard is through steaming. Raise heat to high and add chard with liquid to oil mixture. Stir-fry for about 2 minutes until leaves are thoroughly coated with oil and flavors have blended.

1 bunch swiss chard, chopped
4 cloves of garlic, minced
1 medium onion, diced
1/4 cup olive oil
1/4 cup water

CURTIS'S STUFFED EGGPLANT

1 large eggplant
2 green onions, chopped
4 oz. mushrooms, diced
2 cloves garlic, minced
one-quarter bell pepper, diced
one-quarter fresh pineapple,
    diced
3 oz. chopped nuts
1 oz. each fresh chopped basil
    and marjoram
10 oz. black or red beans
    (1 can)
4 oz. salsa
1 Tbl. oil

Wash eggplant and slice in half lengthwise. Leave cap attached. Scoop out middle leaving eggplant shell about 1/2 inch thick. Place shells in preheated 350 degree oven and bake for 20 minutes. (You can spread the shells with oil to keep them soft.)

Finely dice the flesh that was removed from the eggplant. Sauté diced eggplant, onions, mushrooms, and bell pepper in oil for about 5 minutes. Add tomatoes, pineapple, nuts, herbs, and beans; sauté at least 5 minutes more.

Fill shells with sautéed mixture. Top with salsa and return to oven. Bake 30 to 45 minutes. This dish is great served with white or brown rice.

FRIED EGGPLANT WITH GARLIC SAUCE

GARLIC SAUCE

6 or 7 cloves of garlic,
    chopped
2 Tbl. vinegar
3 Tbl. soy sauce
1 tsp. sugar
1 Tbl. plum jam
1/2 tsp. corn starch

Blend all ingredients well; let stand for 10 minutes while preparing the eggplant.

EGGPLANT

6 Japanese eggplants

Wash and cut at a long angle crosswise. Lightly fry in soy oil, about 3 minutes per side. As the slices brown, remove them to a paper towel to drain. When all slices are done, drain excess oil from pan. Return slices to pan and cover with garlic sauce. Heat through and serve.

AIKENS' VEGETARIAN DRESSING

My mom never made stuffing; she always prepared what we called "dressing" on the side in a large roasting pan. Thanksgiving was turkey dressing, and for after-church dinner it was chicken dressing. I've taken many of Mama's wonderful southern recipes (including hers for dressing) and rewritten them to suit my vegetarian lifestyle. At my house the dressing is no longer a side dish; it has become the center of many family meals.

Boil vegetables in broth 15 to 20 minutes or until tender. Allow to cool enough to handle. Add all additional ingredients to vegetables and broth. Mix well. Put mixture into a large, flat baking dish. Bake at 350 degrees for 40-50 minutes or until golden brown and set in the middle. When a straw inserted at the center comes out clean, the dressing is done.

2 pans cornbread, crumbled
1/2 loaf bread, toasted and crumbled
1/4 package saltine crackers, crumbled
2-1/2 cups vegetable broth
3 large onions, diced
4 ribs celery, diced
3 eggs
1/4 cup buttermilk
1 stick margarine
1 Tbl. sage

MAIN DISHES

FRITTATAS

A Frittata is a mixture of eggs and vegetables rather like an omelet, except that it is cooked on both sides in a deep frying pan. It is served flat, cut into sections for individual portions, and eaten hot or cold as a luncheon main dish with salad or sliced tomatoes, or as a light snack.

THE FAST STOVE TOP FRITTATA

*Warning:
Reads tough,
but easy to do!*

1. As an entrée, either for lunch or dinner, figure about 2-1/2 to 3 eggs per person. Beat eggs together with salt and pepper until frothy. (The French add about one tablespoon of water to two eggs, to make them blend better. I use a little milk.)

2. Using the measure of 1-1/2 teaspoons of oil to 2 eggs, heat oil in skillet over medium setting until hot.

3. Add half of the beaten, seasoned eggs. As they begin to set around the edges, add veggies and start gently lifting egg mixture from sides of pan and push to center, allowing uncooked mixture to contact pan surface.

4. Add remaining beaten eggs. Continue gently moving "set" egg mixture to center—it's self-leveling.

5. As the frittata loses its runniness, place a large plate over the skillet and quickly invert the entire frittata. Slide it back into the pan so the uncooked side is on the bottom and continue cooking until done.

When you insert a wooden toothpick and it comes out clean, it's done. Believe me, do it once and you've mastered it!

THE EASY OVEN FRITTATA

Ideal for Parties!

Preheat oven to 325 degrees. Mix ingredients well and pour into a greased 8-inch square baking pan. Bake 1 hour. Cut into slices or into 1-inch squares for appetizers. Serve hot or cold.

No matter which way you do it, you'll need a non-stick finish pan, a well-seasoned cast-iron pan, or any type of frying pan that is not inclined to stick. Like an omelet, the filling should be cooked before adding it to the egg mixture. There's no better way to use leftovers.
Here are a couple of recipes to get you started:

ARTICHOKE FRITTATA

My mother-in-law served this dish to us at our annual Christmas Tree decorating party in 1992. It's fantastic!

Use either method above for preparation.

Filling:
1 lb. marinated artichokes (recipe on page 184)
1/2 lb. cheddar cheese, grated
1 medium onion, finely chopped
6 saltines, finely crushed

Egg Mixture:
4 eggs, beaten
water or milk
dash of Tabasco sauce
salt and pepper to taste

SPINACH AND ASPARAGUS FRITTATA

Filling:

1 lb. spinach, washed and
   drained with stems
   removed
1 lb. asparagus, cut in
   1-inch pieces
2 cloves garlic, minced or
   mashed

Egg Mixture:

8 eggs, beaten
3 Tbl. whipping cream or
   water
1/4 tsp. salt
pepper to taste
2 Tbl. parmesan or romano
   cheese, shredded
4 Tbl. olive oil

Use either method above for preparation.

RATATOUILLE

(Ex-Girlfriend's Dish)

1 medium eggplant
1 each red and green pepper
1 lb. tomatoes
1 lb. zucchini
1 yellow squash
1 medium Vidalia onion
2 cloves garlic, minced
1/2 cup oil
1/4 cup water
salt and pepper to taste
Don't forget thyme — 1 tsp.

Peel eggplant, squash, and onion. Wash other vegetables and cut everything into 1/2-inch pieces. Place in a big pot and add oil and water. *DON'T FORGET SEASONING.* Cook on medium heat 1-1/2 to 2 hours.

P.S. She and I are still friends.

THE PERFECT BURGER

(Vegetarian)

Sauté onion in margarine until clear. Add celery and carrots. Cook until soft. Cool. Mix with remaining ingredients. Form into patties. Can be fried; however, I feel they come out better when broiled.

1 cup ground walnuts or pecans
half an onion, chopped
1 rib celery, chopped
1 carrot, chopped
1/2 cup seasoned bread crumbs
1/2 cup cooked rice (brown)
2 eggs
salt and pepper to taste

CURTIS AIKENS' PIZZA

THE SUPER SAUCE

(Great for BBQ, Spaghetti, and on Pizza)

Pour first four ingredients in a saucepan. Bring to boil; lower heat. Next ingredients should be chopped very fine or run through a food processor, then added to saucepan. Next add Worcestershire sauce and cook on medium heat 30 to 45 minutes. *If you like it thicker, add 1 tsp. cornstarch.*

3 ripe red tomatoes, diced
juice of half a lemon
3 Tbl. sugar
3 oz. yellow mustard
one-half each red and green pepper
5 cloves garlic
1 medium onion, diced
1-1/2 Tbl. Worcestershire sauce

Curtis Aikens' Pizza Dough

1 package yeast
1/2 tsp. sugar
3/4 cup warm water
2 cups flour
2 Tbl. oil
dash of salt
1 small onion, diced
2 cloves garlic, chopped
2 green onions, chopped
1 oz. each fresh chopped basil,
    thyme, and oregano
Super Sauce *(above)*
your favorite cheese

Pour yeast, sugar, and water into a small bowl. Let stand 10 minutes to proof. Into a large bowl, sift flour and salt; add oil, chopped vegetables, and herbs. If bubbles have formed in the yeast, it has proofed. Add it to flour. Mix well with wooden spoon. When dough forms, knead with hands for about 10 minutes or until smooth. Place dough in lightly oiled bowl for about 30 minutes. It will double in size. Knead it into a small ball; roll out to fit your pizza pan. Cover with Super Sauce and cheese. Bake in 350 degree oven for about 40 minutes or until edges are golden brown.

Deep Dish Pizza Pie

Filling:
4 oz. grated Parmesan cheese
4 oz. cooked chicken,
    chopped
2 tomatoes, diced
2 oz. mozzarella, diced
1 oz. each fresh parsley and
    sage, chopped
2 eggs beaten
5 Tbl. heavy cream
1/8 tsp. nutmeg
salt and pepper to taste

Oil a pizza dish, line with Curtis Aikens' Pizza Dough. Spread half the Parmesan cheese over dough, add chicken and tomatoes. Mix remaining ingredients together. Add to pie. Bake in preheated 375 degree oven 35 to 40 minutes, or until edges are golden brown.

CURTIS AIKENS' VEGETARIAN LASAGNA

Cook pasta. Drain and set aside. Your sauce should be ready. Mix ricotta and margarine together until creamy. Add remaining ingredients and mix. To assemble lasagna, oil a baking dish, place 3 sheets of pasta on the bottom, cover with 1/3 of the sauce, carefully spread a layer of the cheese mixture, 3 more pasta sheets, another 1/3 of the sauce, and the remaining cheese mixture. Cover that with the last 3 pasta sheets. Add the last of the Super Sauce.

Cover with foil and bake in preheated 375 degree oven for 20 minutes. Remove foil. Bake about 10 minutes more. Let cool about 20 minutes before serving.

9 sheets spinach or plain
  lasagna pasta
Super Sauce *(above)*,
  thickened with 1 Tbl.
  cornstarch
1 lb. ricotta cheese
4 Tbl. unsalted margarine
2 cups grated mozzarella
1/8 tsp. nutmeg
salt and pepper to taste

PASTA WITH CHICKEN, ASPARAGUS, AND CREAM SAUCE

Cook noodles in boiling water with 1 tablespoon olive oil for about 15 minutes. Meanwhile, prepare sauce. In a sauté pan, melt margarine. Add chicken, asparagus, and cream. Bring to boil and cook about 5 minutes to thicken sauce. Season to taste with salt and pepper. Drain and rinse pasta. Add sauce and serve.

10 oz. penne noodles
12 oz. stemmed asparagus,
  cut into 1-inch pieces
5 oz. sautéed chicken breast,
  cut into 1-inch pieces
2 Tbl. margarine
1 cup heavy cream

CURTIS'S CHICKEN VEGETABLE LINGUINI

8 oz. chicken, sliced into
   small pieces
2 Tbl. margarine
5 cloves garlic, chopped
1 onion, chopped
half a red pepper, chopped
3 Tbl. flour
1/2 cup milk
Linguini prepared according
   to packaged instructions

In a frying pan, add margarine, sauté chicken, garlic, onions, and bell pepper until vegetables are tender and all pinkness is out of chicken. Add flour and milk. Cook until sauce thickens and becomes smooth. Now serve over linguini.

CURTIS AIKENS' CHICKEN DINNER

1/2 chicken, cut up
2 Tbl. margarine
4 cloves garlic, chopped
1 onion, chopped
half a bell pepper, chopped
1/2 cup seedless grapes,
   sliced
1/2 cup cantaloupe, sliced
   into squares
3 oz. maple syrup
salt and pepper to taste

In a frying pan, sauté garlic and onions in margarine. Add chicken and brown. Add pepper, grapes, melon, and seasoning. Place cover on pan and cook about 25 minutes. Remove lid and pour syrup over chicken. Cook 10 to 15 minutes longer. Serve with rice or baked potato.

ONE PAN TURKEY DINNER

1 lb. ground turkey
1 onion, sliced
1 zucchini, sliced
1 yellow squash, sliced
5 Napa cabbage leaves
season with Jenny's Salad
   Dressing *(recipe on
   page 168)*

Season turkey by mixing with 3 oz. salad dressing. Then form patties and place in a frying pan. Cover turkey with sliced vegetables. Place Napa cabbage on top. Pour 3 oz. dressing over napa. Place lid on pan. Cook on medium heat 25 to 35 minutes.

SIX-LAYER TURKEY DINNER

Sauté all vegetables in white wine for about 3 minutes. Cool.

In a casserole dish, **layer 1:** 1 lb. ground turkey pressed flat; **layer 2:** honey dill mustard; **layer 3:** vegetables; **layer 4:** 1 lb. turkey; **layer 5:** grain mustard; **layer 6:** sliced red apple. Bake in 325 degree oven about 40 minutes.

2 lbs. ground turkey, sautéed
3 oz. honey dill mustard
3 oz. grain mustard
1 onion, chopped
1 Granny Smith apple, chopped
1 each green and red pepper, chopped
2 broccoli tops, chopped
4 Tbl. white wine
1 red apple

ELENEKI CHICKEN

A recipe I learned while vacationing in Hawaii. For a family of 4 Hawaiians (they love to eat).

Step 1.

In a large pot, marinate all items for at least 4 hours (overnight is best). Pour off half the liquid (save it; you may need it during cooking). Cook on high heat about 30 minutes or until chicken is done.

12 chicken thighs, boned and quartered
32 oz. soy sauce
3 cups sugar
3 oz. fresh ginger, grated
4 cloves garlic, chopped
2 large sweet onions, quartered

Step 2.

After chicken is done, lower heat and add second set of ingredients to pot. Cook about 15 minutes longer and serve with rice. You will love it.

8 oz. canned bamboo shoots, sliced
8 oz. long grain rice (soak 30 minutes in warm water)
2 or 3 bunches green onions, chopped
6 oz. fresh mushrooms, sliced
8 oz. tofu, diced
1 package abrage (fried tofu), sliced

TROPICAL CHICKEN

2 Tbl. margarine
8 oz. chicken, diced
1 cup diced pineapple
half a banana, sliced
1 cup diced sweet potato
1/4 cup Worcestershire
    sauce
salt and pepper to taste

Marinate chicken in Worcestershire sauce for about 20 minutes. Then sauté in margarine, until all pinkness is gone. Add potatoes; cook about 4 minutes. Add banana and pineapple. Cook about 2 minutes. Serve over rice.

FISH WITH HERB SAUCE

1 lb. button mushrooms,
    whole
1 clove garlic, chopped
3 tsp. olive oil
juice of 1 lemon
1 Tbl. parsley, chopped
2 tsp. basil, chopped
1 tsp. sage, chopped
4 tsp. white wine mixed with
    1/2 tsp. cornstarch
4 cleaned fish, about 8 oz.
    each
2 tsp. bread crumbs
2 tsp. grated Parmesan
    cheese

In a frying pan, add oil, garlic, and mushrooms. Sauté about 2 minutes. Add herbs, lemon juice, and wine with cornstarch. Bring to boil; cook until it thickens. Set aside. Place fish in a shallow oven dish. Pour sauce over fish. Sprinkle with bread crumbs and cheese. Cover with foil, not too tight, and cook in preheated 375 degree oven about 20 minutes. Remove foil for last 5 minutes of cooking.

AMAZINGLY SIMPLE FISH

In a frying pan, place fish in one layer. Cover with water and add onion, parsley, salt, and peppercorn. Bring to an easy boil; lower heat and simmer 20 minutes. When fish is done, place it on serving plates. In a small pan, brown the margarine; add capers and turn off heat; add vinegar. Pour over fish and serve.

4 boneless pieces of fish
1 slice onion
2 parsley stalks
1/8 tsp. salt
6 black peppercorns
4 Tbl. margarine
2 Tbl. white wine vinegar
1 Tbl. capers

PECAN LOAF A LA MARCIA VAN SUSTEREN

Mix first set of ingredients together and boil for 5 minutes.

2 cups pecans, finely ground
1 large onion, chopped
1 large green pepper, chopped

Mix second set together and hold aside.

2 cups cooked rice
5 Tbl. butter
1/2 cup water

In a large bowl, beat eggs and add both milks. Mix together. Add the pecan and rice mixtures, and the pimiento; stir well. Put all in a greased casserole dish or ring mold. Set the dish in a pan of water and bake at 325 degrees for 1 hour or until firm. Great with a mushroom sauce!

4 eggs
1 large can evaporated milk
1/2 cup sweet milk
1 can pimiento, chopped

SWEET PEPPER SENSATION

3 large red peppers
2 Tbl. olive oil
3-4 cloves of garlic
oil to brush on peppers

Brush each pepper with a bit of oil. Roast in the oven, grill on the stove top, or barbeque until peppers are totally black and ugly. Cool and peel.* Slice and seed the peppers. Purée seeded peppers in a blender with oil and garlic. Heat and serve over pasta or rice. Top with The Perfect Sweet Pepper Sensation Topping, if desired.

*If you allow the peppers to cool inside a sealed paper bag, the skins will slip right off.

THE PERFECT SWEET PEPPER SENSATION TOPPING

one-half each red and green
    pepper, diced
2-3 cloves of garlic, chopped
1 Tbl. olive oil

Sauté peppers and garlic in olive oil. After pouring sauce over your favorite pasta, add topping. Serve and ENJOY!

WOK STEW

If you don't have a wok, a heavy covered skillet will do nicely.

2 to 3 oz. olive oil
1 medium to large eggplant,
    cubed
1 large onion, diced
1/4 lb. asparagus, cut
    into 1-inch pieces
6 leaves Napa cabbage,
    chopped
1 basket of cherry tomatoes,
    sliced in half
oregano
sage
thyme
salt and pepper to taste
round mini-loaves of bread

Sauté eggplant and onion for approximately 4 minutes. Add asparagus and cabbage and cook 4 minutes more. Finally, add tomatoes and seasoning to taste. Place lid on wok. Simmer 10 to 15 minutes.

Hollow out the centers of the mini-loaves. Serve stew in the hollowed-out loaves. Garnish with bread from inside of loaves.

MARINATED K-BOBS

Mix first four ingredients together. Set aside.

1/2 cup olive oil
1 cup fresh pineapple juice
1/3 cup fresh orange juice
1/3 cup fresh soy sauce

On skewers, assemble selection of pearl onions, green and red peppers, broccoli stalks and tops, chunks of tofu, and firm cherry tomatoes. Place K-Bobs in marinade and turn until evenly coated. Place on grill and keep brushing with marinade as you turn them. Grill until they're nicely crisp-browned. Brush with remaining marinade as you remove skewers to serve.

pearl onions
green and red peppers, sliced
broccoli
tofu
cherry tomatoes

MUSSELS MADE EASY

Wash mussels using a scrub brush and remove "beards." Soak in cold water with 3/4 cup of flour for at least 45 minutes. The mussels will spit out any sand they might have taken in and they will plump up.

In a large pot add wine, shallots, and garlic. Bring to boil. Add mussels and cover pot. Cook about 6 minutes. Lift mussels out of pot and place into serving dishes. Discard any mussels which are not open.

Reduce liquid by half and strain into another sauce pan. Add cream and bring to boil to thicken. Add butter and parsley. Season to taste. Pour sauce over mussels and enjoy!

3 lbs. mussels
2 cups white wine
5 shallots, chopped
1 clove of garlic, chopped
1/2 cup cream
3 Tbl. margarine, cut into
    small pieces
2 Tbl. parsley, chopped

BAKED ORANGE ROUGHY AND VEGETABLES

2 lbs. orange roughy

4 oz. fresh ranch dressing

4 oz. each fresh chopped
broccoli, cauliflower,
carrots, squash, and
onion

Wash and pat fish dry, set aside. Steam all vegetables about 2 minutes. Place cooked vegetables on an oiled baking dish. Pour half the dressing over steamed vegetables. Place fish on top of vegetables. Cover with foil and bake in preheated 350 degree oven for about 15 minutes. Remove foil and bake 5 minutes more. Pour remaining dressing over fish and serve.

DESSERTS

TROPICAL CHEESECAKE

(Making this cake is fun; there are three separate parts which must be combined.)

MACADAMIA NUT PIE CRUST

1 cup flour
1 stick margarine
1/4 cup sugar
1/2 cup macadamia nuts,
    chopped

In a large mixing bowl, add all ingredients, cut with pastry knife until everything is mixed (what I call a dry stickie). Place dough in pie pan. Smooth evenly. Bake 20 to 30 minutes at 350 degrees, or until edges are light brown.

PINEAPPLE GLAZE

2-1/2 cups pineapple, diced
1/3 cup sugar
1/3 cup water
1 Tbl. cornstarch

In a small saucepan, add pineapple, sugar, and water. Bring to boil. Lower heat and add cornstarch, stirring constantly until thickened. This glaze is not only good over cheesecake; try it over ice cream, sliced fruit, or toast.

CHEESECAKE FILLING

8 oz. cream cheese
1/3 cup powdered sugar
1 tsp. vanilla
16 oz. whipped topping

In a mixing bowl, add cheese and whip until fluffy; add sugar and whipped topping. Mix until fluffy.

Fill pie shell and top with pineapple glaze and refrigerate. It will be ready to serve in about 30 minutes.

PEACHES STUFFED WITH CHOCOLATE

Place peaches in a large bowl. Add wine, brandy, and enough water to cover peaches. Marinate for an hour. Mix chocolate and egg yolk well; add peach liqueur. Whip the cream and fold into chocolate along with the almonds.

Remove peaches from marinade and place them in serving dish. Spoon chocolate mixture in center of peach and top. Place wafer in center. Chill and serve.

* If unavailable in your area, melt 2 oz. semi-sweet chocolate.

4 large peaches, peeled, sliced in half, and stone removed
1 cup dry white wine
2 Tbl. brandy
2 packs soft semi-sweet chocolate*
1 egg yolk
1 Tbl. ground almonds
1 Tbl. peach liqueur
1/2 cup heavy cream
4 vanilla wafers

GRAND MARNIER PECAN TOPPING

Pour Grand Marnier over pecans. Marinate together at least 12 hours before preparing topping.

To a saucepan, add margarine and drained pecans. Reserve Grand Marnier. Sauté about 40 seconds. Add water and sugar and bring to boil. Stir until mixture thickens. Add Grand Marnier. Cook on high heat about 30 seconds more. Serve over ice cream or cake.

1 cup pecans
1/2 cup Grand Marnier
1/4 stick margarine
1/4 cup water
1/4 cup sugar

MAMA'S PASTRY DOUGH

In a mixing bowl, sift flour. Add shortening and water in small amounts until dough forms. Knead until smooth. Refrigerate until needed.

1-1/2 cups flour
1/2 cup vegetable shortening
1/2 cup cold water

MAMA'S SWEET POTATO PIE

Makes 2 pies.

3 large sweet potatoes,
    peeled, sliced, and boiled
2 sticks margarine
1-1/2 cups sugar
4 eggs, well beaten
1/2 cup buttermilk
1 tsp. vanilla
2 homemade pie crusts

Mash sweet potatoes with margarine while hot. Add sugar and eggs and mix well; then add milk and vanilla and mix again. Pour custard into pie crust. Bake in preheated 300 degree oven for 1 hour, or until a straw inserted in the center comes out clean.

MAMA LAURA AIKENS' PUMPKIN PIE

2 cups cooked and mashed
    pumpkin
1 cup sugar
1/2 stick margarine
3 eggs, beaten
1/2 cup buttermilk
1 Tbl. vanilla
1 tsp. nutmeg
1 tsp. cinnamon
1/2 tsp. fresh lemon juice
1 homemade deep-dish pie
    crust

Mix all ingredients well and add to pie crust. Then bake in preheated 350 degree oven for 1 hour. Cool, slice, and serve. Add whipped cream if you like.

FRESH COCONUT PIE

In a mixing bowl add margarine, sugar, flour, eggs, and buttermilk. Mix well. Add coconut and vanilla. Mix, then pour into pie crust. Bake in preheated 300 degree oven for 1 hour. Cool before serving.

1 cup sugar
1/2 stick melted margarine
2 Tbl. flour
3 eggs
1 tsp. vanilla
1 cup buttermilk
1 cup coconut, grated
1 homemade pie crust

PASSION CHIFFON PIE

Beat egg yolks until thick. Add 1/2 cup sugar, salt, and passion fruit juice. Cook over low heat until thick, stirring constantly. Add gelatin, which has been dissolved in cold water. Add lemon rind and cool until slightly congealed. Beat egg whites with remaining 1/2 cup of sugar. Fold slightly beaten egg whites into cooled yolk mixture. Pour into cool pie shell. Chill until nice and stiff. Serve with whipped cream and enjoy.

4 eggs, separated
1 cup sugar
1/2 tsp. salt
1 cup passion fruit juice
1 tsp. unflavored gelatin
1/4 cup cold water
1 tsp. lemon rind, grated
1 baked pie shell
1/2 cup whipped cream

CHOCOLATE BANANA PIE

Place eggs in a medium saucepan; beat. Add sugar and chocolate. Mix well. Add flour and mix. Add milk and bring to easy boil. Add vanilla, stir, and remove from heat. Add bananas and wafer crumbs; fold into crust. Freeze before serving.

4 bananas, mashed
8 oz. vanilla wafer crumbs
2 eggs
1 cup sugar
1 Tbl. flour
1 oz. soft, unsweetened
    chocolate
2 cups milk
1 tsp. vanilla
1 deep-dish pie crust

MAMA'S SPECIAL BANANA PUDDING

2 to 3 lbs. bananas
1 box vanilla wafers
1 cup sugar
2 Tbl. flour
2 eggs
2 cups milk
1 tsp. vanilla

In a large bowl, place one layer of sliced bananas, then a layer of wafers until bowl is filled, making sure top layer is wafer. Set aside.

In a medium boiler, beat eggs; add sugar. Mix well, then add flour, milk, and vanilla. Bring mixture to boil, being careful not to burn it as it heats. Pour over bananas and wafers. Chill and serve.

APPLE TURNOVERS

(I made these for World Heavyweight Boxing Champ Evander "Real Deal" Holyfield in Reno.)

Mama's Pastry Dough *(recipe on page 205)*
2 to 3 lbs. apples, peeled, cored, and sliced
1 tsp. vanilla
1 cup sugar
1/2 tsp. cinnamon
1/2 tsp. nutmeg
1/2 stick margarine

Section dough into four balls and roll flat. Combine apples, vanilla, sugar, cinnamon, and nutmeg. Fill dough. Add margarine to each turnover. Fold dough over and seal edges. Bake in 400 degree oven for about 20 minutes.

Should make four or five nice-size turnovers.

MAMA'S SIMPLE PEACH COBBLER

(Made in 8-1/2 x 8-1/2 dish, 2" deep)

7 or 8 medium peaches, peeled and sliced
1 cup sugar
1 Tbl. flour
2 Tbl. vanilla
1-1/2 cups water
1/2 stick margarine
1 homemade crust

Place sliced peaches in a baking dish. Pour sugar over them, then flour. Add vanilla and water. Mix just a little. Slice margarine and arrange over peaches. Place crust on top. Bake in 350 degree oven for 45 minutes.

GEORGIA PEACH OF A PIE

PIE

Bake pie crust until light brown; set aside. In a small saucepan, add peaches, raw sugar, and water. Cook about 6 minutes (keep that juice for glaze). Set aside.

Combine cream cheese, milk, almond extract, and sugar. Mix until smooth; spread into pie crust. Cover with peaches and glaze *(glaze recipe follows)*. Chill and serve.

1 deep-dish pie crust
3 to 4 lbs. fresh peaches, peeled and sliced
2 Tbl. raw sugar
1 cup water
16 oz. cream cheese
4 Tbl. milk
1/2 tsp. almond extract
4 Tbl. sugar

GLAZE

Combine cornstarch and sugar in a saucepan. Add lemon juice and peach juice, stirring over medium heat until clear and thick. Add margarine; cool and pour over peaches.

1 Tbl. cornstarch
1/4 cup sugar
1 Tbl. lemon juice
2/3 cup peach juice *(from above)*
1 Tbl. margarine

E-Z CRANBERRY PIE

Mix all ingredients, then add to pie crust. Add top crust and prick with fork. Preheat oven to 450 degrees and bake pie 10 minutes. Lower temperature to 350 degrees. Bake 40 minutes more.

3-1/2 cups cranberries, chopped
1-1/2 cups sugar
1-1/2 Tbl. flour
1/4 tsp. salt
3 Tbl. water
3 Tbl. melted butter or margarine
1 9-inch pie crust and 1 crust for top *(or Mama's Pastry Dough, page 205)*

MACADAMIA NUT PIE

3 eggs
1 cup light corn syrup
2/3 cup sugar
1/4 cup melted margarine
4 Tbl. dark rum
1 Tbl. vanilla
1 cup macadamia nuts,
    chopped
1 homemade pie crust

Beat together eggs, sugar, syrup, and margarine. Add rum and vanilla. Mix and add nuts. Turn into pie crust. Bake at 375 degrees until filling sets, about 45 minutes. Cool and serve.

SORBET AND FRENCH PEARS

1 basket fresh raspberries
1 oz. honey
juice of 2 oranges
4 Comice pears
2 cups fresh mixed fruits,
    diced

Pour berries and honey into a blender and purée. Pour into a saucepan and heat. Peel and core pears; place in a boiler. Add orange juice. Bring to boil and remove from heat. To serve, arrange diced fruits on serving plates. Place pear on top. Cover with orange juice. Cover that with the berry mixture.

DESSERT PIZZA

1 pizza crust *(recipe on
    page 194)*
1 cup fresh crushed
    pineapple
2 to 4 oz. cheese, grated
1 to 2 Tbl. margarine
2 Tbl. brown sugar
1/4 tsp. cinnamon
1 small apple, cored and
    sliced
1 pear, cored and sliced
2 oz. Kahlua

Season pizza dough with just a bit of cinnamon. Use crushed pineapple as sauce. In a saucepan melt margarine, add sugar and remaining cinnamon. Add apples, pears, and Kahlua. Sauté about 4 minutes.

Top pizza dough with sautéed fruit and grated cheese. Bake in preheated 400 degree oven for 35 to 45 minutes.

PINEAPPLE CARAMEL

In a saucepan combine margarine, sugar, and cream. Stir over heat until sugar dissolves and mixture thickens, about 3 minutes. Add pecans. Spoon over pineapple and serve.

1 fresh pineapple, sliced and diced
1/3 cup brown sugar
1/3 cup margarine
1/3 cup heavy cream
1/4 cup pecans, chopped

GEORGIA TO GEORGIA TEA CAKE

First cream the margarine and sugar. Then add flour, salt, and vanilla. Mix well. Add nuts, then mix. Spread coconut over working space. Roll mixture in coconut until it forms a log. Chill.

Preheat oven to 325 degrees. Cut tea log into 1- to 2-inch pieces. Roll into balls, place on cookie sheet, and bake 15 to 19 minutes. Cover with powdered sugar.

1 cup margarine
1/2 cup powdered sugar
2-1/4 cups flour
1/4 tsp. salt
1 tsp. vanilla
1/2 cup walnuts, chopped
1/2 cup pecans
1/2 cup fresh coconut

CHOCOLATE PECAN ZUCCHINI BUNDT CAKE

Mix first 4 ingredients and set aside. In a mixing bowl, beat eggs and add sugar, 1/4 cup at a time. Add chocolate mix, then add oil. Add flour mixture and blend well. Fold in zucchini and pecans. Mix well. Fold into bundt pan. Bake in preheated 350 degree oven for 1 hour and 15 minutes. Cool 15 minutes before removing cake from pan. Sprinkle powdered sugar on cake and serve.

3 cups flour
1-1/2 tsp. baking powder
1 tsp. baking soda
1 tsp. salt
4 eggs
3 cups sugar
3 packs soft baking chocolate
   (or 3 squares, melted)
1-1/2 cups oil
3 cups grated zucchini
1 cup pecans, chopped
3 Tbl. powdered sugar

APPLE MUFFINS

3/4 cup cooking oil
1 cup sugar
2 eggs
1-1/2 cups flour
1 tsp. salt
1 tsp. baking soda
1 tsp. vanilla
1 tsp. cinnamon
2 apples, peeled and diced

Combine oil, sugar, and egg. Mix well. Blend in flour, salt, baking soda, cinnamon, and vanilla. Stir in fresh apples. Pour into muffin pan. Bake at 350 degrees 10 to 15 minutes.

ORANGE MUFFINS

3/4 cup cooking oil
1 cup sugar
2 eggs
1-1/2 cups flour
1 tsp. salt
1 tsp. baking soda
1 tsp. vanilla
1/4 cup fresh orange juice
2 Tbl. grated orange rind

Combine oil, sugar, and eggs. Mix well. Add remaining ingredients. Blend. Pour into muffin pan. Bake at 350 degrees for 10 to 15 minutes.

CHOCOLATE CREPES WITH STRAWBERRY JAM

Batter:
1-1/2 cups milk and water
    mixed
4 eggs
1/8 tsp. salt
2 cups flour, sifted
1 Tbl. sugar
4 Tbl. melted margarine

Filling:
8 oz. semi-sweet chocolate,
    grated
4 oz. strawberry jam
whipped cream
toasted pecans

In a large bowl, add batter ingredients. Mix well until creamy batter forms. To cook: brush crepe or small frying pan with oil over high heat. Add large spoonful of batter. Swirl in pan to cover base. Pour off excess batter. Brown one side, then the other. As crepes are cooked, spread jam and chocolate on one side of the fold. Repeat this until all batter is cooked. Makes at least 12 crepes. Divide into serving size. Top with whipped cream and nuts.

BREADSTUFFS

POTATO PANCAKES

3 medium raw potatoes
1 small onion
1 egg
2 Tbl. flour
dash of pepper
1/2 tsp. salt
1/4 tsp. baking powder

Peel and grate potatoes and onion. Let stand 10 to 15 minutes, then pour off liquid. Add remaining ingredients and mix well. Drop by spoonfuls into a hot oiled skillet and fry three to four minutes on each side. Great with apple butter, apple sauce, or sour cream.

GERMAN APPLE PANCAKES

1 cup sifted flour
1/2 tsp. baking powder
pinch of salt
1 cup milk
5 eggs
2 Tbl. melted butter
2 medium apples, sliced thin
    and sautéed in butter

Mix dry ingredients. Stir in milk. Add eggs one at a time and beat into batter. Add melted butter. Pour in a hot oiled skillet. Then bake in 425 degree oven until puffed and golden brown, 20 to 25 minutes.
Serve hot with sautéed apples on top.

BANANA BREAD

2 eggs, beaten
1/2 cup melted margarine
3 ripe bananas, mashed
1 cup sugar
1/2 cup flour
1/2 tsp. salt
1 tsp. baking soda
1-1/2 cups whole wheat
    flour
1/2 cup hot water

Mix eggs, margarine, sugar, and bananas. Add flour. Mix. Add remaining ingredients one at a time, mixing well with each addition until batter has thickened. For Quick Bread, pour in wide pan and bake at 375 degrees for 15 to 20 minutes. For loaf, pour into loaf pan. Bake 60 minutes, longer if needed.

MAMA'S CORNBREAD WITH A TOUCH OF CURTIS

Preheat oven to 350 degrees. Mix all ingredients together. Pour some oil into a heavy cast iron skillet or your favorite baking pan and put into oven to heat. When oil is hot, pour prepared batter into center of pan. Bake until lightly browned, about 25-30 minutes.

1-1/2 cup self-rising cornmeal
1/2 cup self-rising flour
3/4 to 1 cup buttermilk
2 eggs, beaten
1/4 cup corn oil
1/2 cup corn kernels
1 bunch green onions, diced
half a red pepper, diced
1/2 cup cheddar cheese chunks
2 jalapeños, diced *(optional)*
fresh herbs, if desired

General Index

RECIPE INDEX